Alexander Pacha

Aus der Reihe: e-fellows.net stipendiaten-wissen

e-fellows.net (Hrsg.)

Band 1257

Sensor Fusion for Robust Outdoor Augmented Reality Tracking on Mobile Devices

GRIN Publishing

Bibliographic information published by the German National Library:

The German National Library lists this publication in the National Bibliography; detailed bibliographic data are available on the Internet at http://dnb.dnb.de .

Imprint:

Copyright © 2013 GRIN Verlag GmbH
Print and binding: Books on Demand GmbH, Norderstedt Germany
ISBN: 978-3-656-96402-5

This book at GRIN:

http://www.grin.com/en/e-book/299825/sensor-fusion-for-robust-outdoor-augmented-reality-tracking-on-mobile-devices

GRIN - Your knowledge has value

Since its foundation in 1998, GRIN has specialized in publishing academic texts by students, college teachers and other academics as e-book and printed book. The website www.grin.com is an ideal platform for presenting term papers, final papers, scientific essays, dissertations and specialist books.

Visit us on the internet:

http://www.grin.com/

http://www.facebook.com/grincom

http://www.twitter.com/grin_com

INSTITUT FÜR SOFTWARE & SYSTEMS
ENGINEERING
Universitätsstraße 6a   D-86135 Augsburg

Sensor fusion for robust outdoor Augmented Reality tracking on mobile devices

Beginn der Arbeit: 05. 07. 2013
Abgabe der Arbeit: 20. 12. 2013

Abstract

Augmented Reality (AR) is the synthesis of virtual and real information in real-time. Visual Augmented Reality allows us to see things that can not be seen with the naked eye. It could be a building that was destroyed in an earthquake with the *CityViewAR* application, a reconstruction of a historical place like in the *Goldfields Explorer* or the virtual topography of a sandbox.

This thesis deals with the question how to best track the position and orientation of a mobile device (smartphone or tablet PC), especially for being used in Augmented Reality. Simple systems use marker-based tracking where an artificial marker is extracted from the camera image and the relative position to it gets estimated. More sophisticated systems fuse visual tracking with additional sensors to achieve the best possible results.

As part of my research, existing systems that implement AR on mobile device were evaluated. Based on these insights, a new sensor fusion approach was developed, implemented for the Android platform and evaluated against other systems. In contrast to many other systems, this new approach is based on existing infrastructure and tries to improve it. The sensors that are usually available in modern smartphones and tablets are a gyroscope, an accelerometer and a compass. Data from all these sensors were combined in a statistical Kalman filter to create virtual sensors, such as a calibrated gyroscope and an orientation-sensor. The calibrated gyroscope operates with high precision and an excellent dynamic response whereas the orientation sensor delivers absolute orientation with respect to gravity and magnetic north. These two virtual sensors were fused in two different ways and achieve stable and robust results that deviate from the reality only 10 degrees on average for normal usage while experiencing virtually no latency.

The outcome of this work is integrated into the Mobile AR Framework which is being developed by the HitLab NZ. On top of this, the cultural heritage application Goldfields Explorer was created that provides information on the Otago Goldfields, a region in New Zealand that was once inhabited by gold-miners but where only ruins remain.

The new approach represents a big improvement regarding reactivity and stability compared to the existing method of the Mobile AR Framework but still has its limitations. It only measures the absolute orientation but not the position of the device; to still obtain a position estimation, the built-in GPS receiver is utilised. Further improvements could be achieved by incorporating computer vision techniques; but due to the technical complexity, only a primitive proof-of-concept prototype was created. Still, the available CV methods were evaluated against a test-data-set and show which algorithms are usable for running on mobile devices and which are computationally too expensive.

Kurzfassung

Augmented Reality (AR) ist die Synthese von virtuellen und realen Informationen in Echtzeit. Mit Visual Augmented Reality können wir Dinge sehen, die für das freie Auge nicht sichtbar sind, egal ob es sich um Gebäude handelt, die durch Erdbeben zerstört wurden wie in der Anwendung *CityViewAR*, Rekonstruktionen von historischen Orten wie im *Goldfields Explorer* oder um eine virtuelle Topographie in einer Sandkiste.

Diese Arbeit beschäftigt sich damit, wie man die Position und Lage eines mobilen Gerätes (Smartphone oder Tablet) bestmöglich verfolgen kann, insbesonders für Augmented Reality. Hierfür gibt es viele Ansätze, reichend von einfachem Marker-Tracking, wo aus dem Kamerabild ein künstlicher Marker extrahiert und die relative Lage zu diesem im Raum bestimmt wird bis zu ausgefeilten Systemen, die Visual-Tracking mit zusätzlichen Sensoren vereinen um möglichst gute Ergebnisse zu erzielen.

Im Rahmen des Forschungspraktikums wurden bestehende Systeme evaluiert, die AR auf mobilen Geräten umsetzen. Darauf aufbauend wurde ein verbesserter Sensorfusionsansatz entwickelt, auf der Androidplattform implementiert und gegen bestehende Systeme evaluiert. Dieser neue Ansatz baut im Gegensatz zu vielen anderen Systemen auf bereits existierender Infrastruktur auf und verbessert diese. Die in modernen Smartphones und Tablets verfügbaren Sensoren: Gyroskop, Akzelerometer sowie Kompass werden in einem statistischen Kalmanfilter vereint um virtuelle Sensoren, wie einen kalibrierten Gyroskopsensor, sowie einen Lagesensor zu erhalten. Der kalibrierte Gyroskopsensor liefert exzellente Reaktionszeiten und hohe Präzision, während der Orientierungssensor eine absolute Messung der Lage im Raum hinsichtlich Gravitation und dem Magnetfeld der Erde liefert. Beide virtuelle Sensoren wurden in zwei verschiedenen Verfahren miteinander kombiniert und liefern bei normaler Nutzung stabile und robuste Ergebnisse, die durchschnittlich nur etwa 10 Grad von der Realität abweichen und dabei kaum Latenz aufweisen.

Die Resultate dieser Arbeit sind im Mobile AR Framework integriert, welches vom Hitlab NZ entwickelt wird. Darauf aufbauend wurde die Kulturerbe-Applikation *Goldfields Explorer* entwickelt, die Informationen zu den in Neuseeland liegenden Otago Goldfeldern liefert, wo früher nach Gold gesucht wurde, heute aber nur noch Ruinen übrig sind.

Das neues System stellt eine große Verbesserung hinsichtlich Reaktionsfähigkeit und Stabilität zu dem bestehendem Verfahren des Mobile AR Frameworks dar, hat aber immer noch gewisse Schwächen. So wird zwar die absolute Lage, jedoch nicht die Position mit diesem Ansatz ermittelt. Dafür wird weiter ausschließlich das GPS-Signal verwendet. Auch die Möglichkeit, das Verfahren mit Hilfe von Computergrafik weiter zu verbessern wurde aufgrund technischer Komplexität über einen primitiven Prototypen hinaus nicht weiter umgesetzt. Die zur Verfügung stehenden Computergrafikverfahren wurden dennoch anhand eines Testdatensatzes evaluiert und zeigen, welche Algorithmen für den Einsatz auf mobilen Geräten geeignet sind, und welche nicht.

Contents

List of Figures

List of Tables

1 Introduction

1.1 Motivation

Augmented Reality(AR) is the synthesis of real and virtual information. AR on hand-held devices such as smartphones or tablets can be used for a variety of applications. For example, the CityViewAR [Lee.2012] lets the user have a look at what Christchurch looked like before the earthquakes in 2010 and 2011 or the Archeoguide [Vlahakis.2002] was an early approach to use AR for archaeology and cultural heritage on Greece's Olympia archaeological site.

But all applications share a common challenge: A robust registration to prevent misaligned virtual objects and robust tracking of the pose and the environment to immerse the user into the application. The stable and robustly aligned rendering of virtual objects in real-time, even if the user is undergoing rapid movement is essential to create a realistic and satisfying user-experience.

Recent developments made smartphones and tablet-PCs reasonable devices for Augmented Reality (see chapter 2) and the ongoing research in this field produced good methods for a robust tracking for AR applications by fusing data from inertial sensors like accelerometer, gyroscope and compass (often summarised as Inertial Measurement Unit (IMU)) and visual tracking (see chapter 3). However, as of today many mobile AR applications are still either marker-based or rely on the sole use of GPS and inertial sensor data [Lee.2012, S. 97] which results in a perception of "floating" objects that are not stable (see figure 1.1). This is a result of the poor quality of the sensors built into mobile phones. But sensors have different problems and if fused together can compensate for the limitations of the other ones. [Furht.2011, S. 14] claims that - in theory - a hybrid system delivers the best results.

1.2 Goals

This work tries to explore the fusion of data from different sensors such as GPS and camera with inertial sensors like accelerometer, gyroscope and compass on mobile devices to create a user-friendly outdoor-AR experience. Based on an in-depth evaluation of existing systems, the goal is to improve the tracking in a way that once an object is placed in the scene, it should stick there no matter what movement the user is undergoing.

Different approaches have been proposed to perform stable tracking on PCs starting with simple marker-based systems to highly complex ones that reconstruct the scene from multiple images while tracking the motion simultaneously, but it is un-

Figure 1.1: "Floating objects" effect in the CityViewAR application caused by sole use of GPS and inertial sensors: Rendered object moves slowly from right to left without a viewpoint change.

clear which strategy works best on mobile devices.

This list of research issues states prominent and important questions from the field of mobile Augmented Reality that are answered throughout this thesis. They were stated at the beginning and refined during my research.

1. What is the current state-of-the-art for Augmented Reality, especially mobile AR? What technologies are being used and what are their limitations? See chapter 3

2. What are the common problems for mobile AR applications? See chapter 3

3. What are the requirements that must be met, when designing a mobile AR application for the mass-market? See chapter 4

4. How to improve tracking on mobile devices? What is a good process to achieve stable tracking? See chapter 5

5. What is the best fusion strategy? And is the fusion of inertial data and visual tracking (hybrid model) a robust and appropriate solution for mobile AR? Or is another approach (good visual tracking, good IMU-tracking) preferable? See chapters 6 and 7

1.3 Structure

The remainder of this thesis is structured as the following: Chapter 2 gives an introduction to the fundamentals of Augmented Reality, sensors, sensor fusion and Computer Vision to help the reader understand the concepts discussed in this thesis. Chapter 3 contains a literature review of scientific work from the field of (Mobile) Augmented Reality to identify the current state-of-the-art in this research area.

Chapter 4 presents a typical use-case where the results from this thesis can be applied to, including a description of the mobile AR application that was developed during the research. Chapter 5 investigates the question, which sensor fusion approach works best on mobile devices and explains in detail the solution approach with the steps that were taken, the techniques that were evaluated and the tools that were used. In chapter 6 the evaluation and results of different CV algorithms as well as of the newly proposed sensor fusion approach are presented and discussed. Finally chapter 7 concludes the thesis by recapitulating the results and describing the future work.

2 Fundamentals

This chapter is dedicated to the fundamentals of Augmented Reality, sensors, sensor fusion and Computer Vision that are used in this thesis to help the reader understand the concepts discussed throughout this work.

2.1 Augmented Reality

Augmented Reality (AR) is a real-time direct or indirect view of physical real-world environment that has been enhanced/augmented by adding virtual computer-generated information to it. [Furht.2011, S. 3]

Augmented reality is often classified into the virtuality continuum, defined by [Milgram.1994]: AR is defined closer to the real environment, whereas Augmented Virtuality (AV) is closer to a purely virtual environment (see figure 2.1).

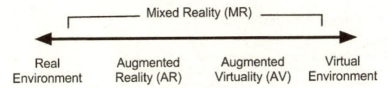

Figure 2.1: Virtuality Continuum by [Milgram.1994]

In other words, Augmented Reality adds virtual information to the immediate surrounding or to any indirect view of the user to enhance the user's perception of and interaction with the real world [Furht.2011, S. 3]. AV in contrast enhances a virtual world with real-world information and is therefore closer to a virtual environment. Virtual Reality (VR) finally immerses the user completely into a virtual environment without seeing the real world.

The first appearance of Augmented Reality dates back to the 1950 [Furht.2011, S. 4], meaning that it has been subject of study for over 60 years. Back then, some researchers defined AR in way that it required the use of a Head-Mounted Display (HMD) [Azuma.1997, S. 2]. Azuma broadened that definition to not limit AR to a specific technology by defining it with the following three characteristics [Azuma.1997, S. 2]:

- Combines real and virtual

- Interactive in real-time

- Registered in 3-D

The third characteristic was clearly stated due to the fact that Augmented Reality was associated with visual augmentation only. But AR is not limited to it; in fact, it can apply all senses, augmenting touch ([Eck.2013], [Sodhi.2013]), hearing or even smelling [Furht.2011]. Nevertheless, the remainder of this thesis will deal only with visual augmentation. When talking about 3D, the Degrees-of-Freedom (DOF) of a system is a central characteristic. It refers to the possible motions of a rigid body and describes whether the system can cope with three axis only either orientation (roll, pitch and yaw) or position (longitude, latitude and altitude) then it is has 3-DOF or six axis (both orientation and position), then it has 6-DOF.

While [Azuma.1997] identified the following six rather specific categories of Augmented Reality applications: medical, manufacturing and repair, annotation and visualisation, robot path planning, entertainment and military aircraft, [Furht.2011, S. 20] re-categorises them into these five, more extendible categories: advertising, entertainment and education, navigation and information, medical and general.

AR systems consist of the following four components: input devices, tracking, computers and displays, which are described in the following in more detail.

2.1.1 Input Devices

Input devices allow the user to interact with an AR system. It can be a glove (Fig. 2.2 left), a wireless wristband (Fig. 2.2 right) or simply the handheld device itself, such as a smartphone [Furht.2011, S. 12]. Smartphones offer multiple ways of interacting: as touch-input, as pointing device (e.g. Google Sky Maps[1]) or even combinations of both as in [Lindeman.2012]s GeoBoids game.

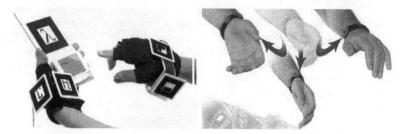

Figure 2.2: Different input devices for AR systems: glove as used by [Reitmayr.2003] (left) and wristband as used by [Feldman.2005] (right)

---

[1]Google Sky Maps: http://www.google.com/mobile/skymap/

2.1.2 Tracking Devices

Tracking devices are used for tracking the user's position and motion. For example video cameras, GPS sensors, accelerometers or wireless sensors are frequently used for tracking. But also any other optical sensors, solid state compasses, gyroscopes or ultrasound-sensors can be used. [Rolland.2001] gives an extensive survey of tracking technologies, classified by their principles of operation. [Papagiannakis.2008] and [Furht.2011] compare different tracking technologies and conclude that a hybrid approach, that combines multiple sensor types is the most promising approach.

2.1.3 Computers

The computer processes the data received from the input device and the tracking device to augment the virtual object correctly. Sufficient computational power and optimised algorithms are essential to meet the real-time requirement. Smartphones and tablets are computers as well but are significantly slower than modern desktop PCs, which directly affects the frame-rate that can be displayed to the user and therefore the user-experience. Slow frame-rates cause a jolting AR experience which destroys the impression of real-time augmentation. [Livingston.2008] conducted a user-study to see the effects of registration errors in Augmented Reality. They showed that latency had a significant effect on the localisation of targets. Neil Trevett, former president of the Web3D consortium and current president of the Khronos Group[2] said at the insideAR conference 2012 in Munich: *"If we turn on all gates (transistors) at the same time, we would blow up the CPU"*, explaining the issue that the computational power of mobile devices is mainly limited by the power consumption and heat production. To solve this conflict between saving battery and high computation power, highly optimised software and hardware is required.

2.1.4 Displays

The results from the previous step are displayed to the user on one of the displays from the following list, which is an extension of the list provided by [Furht.2011, S. 9–12] including examples of recent devices for each category:

- **Retinal Displays / Eye-worn Displays**:
    - Retinal Displays: Displays that utilise lasers to project an image directly onto the user's retina which results in brighter and higher resolution images with a wider field of view than screen-based displays [Lewis.2004], [Bimber.2006], e.g. Virtual Retinal Display developed by the Human Interface Technology Laboratory Washington[3]
    - Contact lenses: Displays which are directly built into a contact lense that can be worn directly in the user's eye, e.g. liquid crystal based

---

[2]Khronos Group: http://www.khronos.org/
[3]Virtual Retinal Display: http://www.hitl.washington.edu/publications/p-95-1/

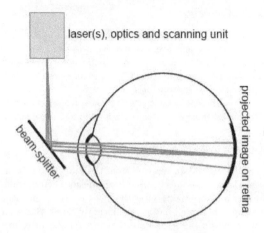

Figure 2.3: Diagram of a retinal display by [Bimber.2006, S. 2]

contact lense by University Gent[4], [Brown.2006]'s Magic Lenses or Randy Sprague's iOptic[5]. These displays were developed recently and are still at an experimental stage because many mechanical, electrical and safety issues remain unsolved.

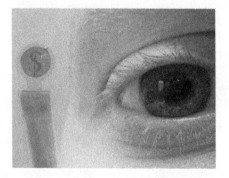

Figure 2.4: AR contact lense by University Gent

[4]Liquid crystal contact lense: http://www.ugent.be/en/news/bulletin/augmented-reality-contact-lens
[5]iOptic contact lense: http://www.popsci.com/diy/article/2012-05/2012-invention-awards-augmented-reality-contact-lenses

- **Head-mounted displays**: Displays which are worn on the head or as a part of a helmet and allow the user to freely use his hands. They can be categorised into monocular or binocular display optics and optical or video see-through displays.

  - **Optical see-through displays**: A display which uses half-silvered mirrors to superimpose computer generated objects directly onto the user's field of view [Milgram.1994], e.g. Google Glasses[6], Vuzix M100[7] or Recon Jet[8]. The main challenges of optical see-through AR systems is to align virtual and real objects in real-time. Figure 2.5 illustrates the principles of optical see-through displays.

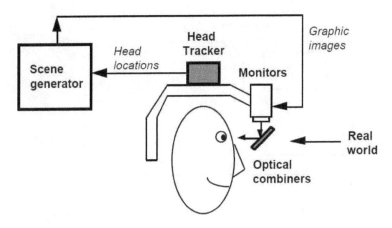

Figure 2.5: Optical see-through conceptual diagram by [Azuma.1997, S. 11]

Although Google Glasses are hyped even before officially released, they are particularly ill-suited for Augmented Reality, where virtual models are overlaid onto the real world camera image, since the display is quite small and positioned outside of the user's main field of view. This has two major implications: Looking at the display is tiresome because the user has to look "up" to focus the display and it is therefore not recommended to look at it for a longer period of time and secondly, the perfect alignment of virtual and real objects is almost impossible. Nevertheless, AR on Glasses is actively being researched[9].

---

[6]Google Glasses: http://www.google.com/glass/start/
[7]Vuzix M100: http://www.vuzix.com/consumer/products_m100.html
[8]Recon Jet: http://jet.reconinstruments.com/
[9]Augmented Reality for Glass: http://arforglass.org/

- **Video see-through displays**: A display where the user only sees the world through the display, e.g. Sony's HMZ-T2[10] or Oculus Rift[11]. These displays are immersive and frequently used in Virtual Reality. Figure 2.6 illustrates the principles of video see-through displays. The advantages of a video see-through display are that the alignment of virtual objects with the reality can be performed very precisely but the full immersion into the system does not allow the user to escape with his eyes. This might lead to motion-sickness with similar symptoms as sea-sickness because the felt motion does not match the visual motion.

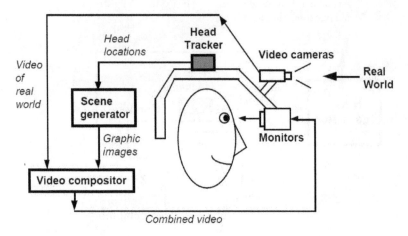

Figure 2.6: Video see-through conceptual diagram by [Azuma.1997, S. 11]

- **Hand-held displays**: Displays that employ small computing devices with a video see-through technique, that the user can hold in his hand. They can be classified into the three categories: smartphone, tablet PC and Personal Digital Assistant (PDA) (which are disappearing from the market due to the dominance of smartphones).

- **Spatial Displays**: Devices that are completely detached from the user, displaying the virtual information directly in the real world with a projector, optical elements, holograms or radio frequency tags, e.g. Augmented Reality Sandbox [Bimber.2006, S. 2].

---

[10]Sony HMZ-T2: http://www.sony.co.uk/hub/personal-3d-viewer
[11]Oculus Rift: http://www.oculusvr.com/

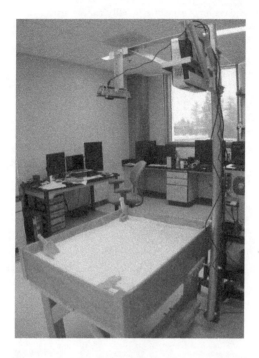

Figure 2.7: Augmented Reality sandbox that uses a projector to augment a relief map and water onto the sand to emphasise the current topography.

The different displays for Augmented Reality can be arranged into the hierarchy given in figure 2.8 ordered by the distance from the eye and the real object.

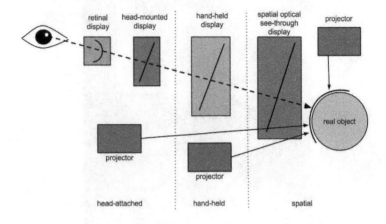

Figure 2.8: Display hierarchy for Augmented Reality as identified by [Bimber.2006]

2.2 Sensors

Modern smartphones and tablets are being shipped with a variety of sensors that can be utilised for Augmented Reality, including

- A (single) back-faced **camera** which can be used for a drift-free visual tracker or simply for creating a video see-through display.

- **GPS sensor** to retrieve the absolute user-position (longitude, latitude, altitude and bearing) up to a certain precision, in the best case a 5m-radius.

- **Magnetic Sensor** that measures magnetic fields surrounding it, including the magnetic field of the earth but also noise from nearby electronic devices that are emitting a magnetic field.

- **3-axis Gyroscope** that measures angular velocities; it and can be used to observe changes in the three rotational axis of the device (yaw, pitch and roll).

- **3-axis Accelerometers** to measure the total external specific forces applied to it [JeroenHol.2008]. This includes accelerations and gravity.

Apart from these hardware sensors, the following derived sensors, also called virtual sensors are available, mostly implemented in software:

- **Gravity**: By combining gyroscope and accelerometer a gravity sensor can be obtained, which gives a precise, drift-free measurement in which direction gravity forces are applied. The way such fusion works best is if it mainly takes data from the gyroscope but corrects drift with the accelerometer.

- **North**: The magnetic compass measures the magnetic field surrounding it, but the magnetic north is not everywhere on the world exactly the same as the true north. This phenomenon is called magnetic declination. In New Zealand for example, the declination is between 18° and 25°. This is especially relevant because the sensor fusion output points towards magnetic north as well. Since the declination is fairly static, the true north can easily be determined, if an approximate position and time is known (e.g. from the GPS sensor).

- **Orientation**: By integrating the data obtained from the gyroscope, angular velocities can be transformed into an orientation. Unfortunately this integration step transforms noise into drift. Secondly - unless initialised - this sensor can only produce a relative orientation estimation.

- **Absolute Orientation**: The most powerful output of IMU sensor fusion, namely an absolute orientation according to the world magnetic field and gravity. To achieve this, gyroscope, accelerometer and compass have to be fused together, where gyroscope gives orientation (in a dynamic response), accelerometer provides correction in terms of gravity and compass provides correction in terms of magnetic north. On the Android platform, this type of sensor is referred to as Rotation Vector[12]. This fusion can be performed with simple high- and low-pass filters or by modelling the dynamics in a Kalman filter.

- **Linear Acceleration**: Theoretically by taking accelerometer data and removing gravity one would obtain linear acceleration. Unfortunately this means that double integration is required, which results in an unbounded position error [Bleser.2009]. Especially if the gravity measurement contains an error in the angle, this method will integrate a constant and heavily drift off [Harris.2013].

Figure 2.9 shows the relationship between hardware and virtual sensors and which sensors are used to obtain the respective virtual sensor.

---

[12] Android Rotation Vector: `http://developer.android.com/guide/topics/sensors/sensors_motion.html#sensors-motion-rotate`

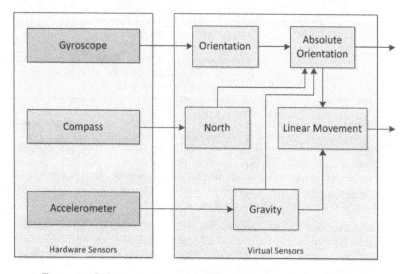

Figure 2.9: Relationship between hardware sensors and virtual sensors.

The following sensors are usually available and could be used to enhance the system even further, but are currently discarded because they are dependent on the availability of infrastructure at the target location:

- **Wi-Fi**: Is being used in urban environments, where a lot of Wi-Fis are surrounding the user. Google Location API uses this approach to improve location and reduce power-consumption by automatically switching between different position-providers (Wi-Fi-positioning or GPS positioning).

- **Cellular Network** (GSM, GPRS, EDGE, UMTS, HSDPA, LTE): [Schall.2009] used a 3G modem in conjunction with a DGPS receiver to reduce influences such as ionospheric or tropospheric effects. These data were provided by the Austrian Positioning Service.

Newer devices ship with even more sensors, that might be useful to create even higher-level virtual sensors. An example of such a higher-level sensor is an activity-sensor to dim the background light, if the user is not looking at the display or detecting whether the user is walking, standing still or driving a car. These sensors are listed here for the sake of completeness, although they are not used:

- **Light sensors** that detect incoming light intensity in Lux.

- **Proximity sensors** that use the light sensor to detect whether the user is currently holding the device next to his ear or not.

- **Front-faced cameras** that directly grab an image of the user, looking at the screen.

- **Microphones** that can record sound and allow the device to hear the surrounding

- **Thermometers** that measure the ambient room temperature. Although it does not seem to be relevant, the environment temperature has an impact on many sensors by causing microscopic physical changes that result in biased measurements.

- **Barometers** that measure air pressure and can be used to correct altitude measurements. This is particularly interesting if a non-planar system should be designed where the altitude needs to be determined precisely.

- **Hygrometers** that measure the humidity of the environment.

2.3 Inertial Sensor Fusion

Hardware sensors such as the accelerometer, the compass or the gyroscope are barely ever used directly, because of noise, drift and deviation. So different sensors that complement one another are usually fused and the result is being used.

2.3.1 Representations

Two sensors, that output a 3D-rotation can easily be fused together if the correct representation is chosen. Different formats can be used to represent a rotation of a rigid body in the 3D-space:

- **Euler-Angles**: Three rotations-angles (yaw, pitch and roll) along predefined axis. Euler-Angles have the benefit of being easy to interpret, but suffer from certain limitations, such as gimbal lock or the lack of the possibility to interpolate between two rotations described in Euler-Angles.

- **Rotation Vector**: A more general form that can represent an arbitrary rotation by specifying a rotation-axis with three components x, y, z and a rotation angle α around this axis.[13]

- **Rotation Matrix**: A 3x3 matrix that can be used directly for rendering rotations. It is very often used in computer graphics, because it can be combined with other transformations and efficiently applied by parallel multiplications.

---

[13] The rotation-vector-representation is - despite the name - different from the Android Orientation Sensor called *Rotation Vector* which uses Quaternion as output format

- **Quaternions**: A closely related representation to the rotation vector; when given a rotation angle and rotation axis x, y, z, quaternions represent them as $q = \cos(\frac{\alpha}{2}) + i(x \cdot \sin(\frac{\alpha}{2})) + j(y \cdot \sin(\frac{\alpha}{2})) + k(z \cdot \sin(\frac{\alpha}{2}))$. On the first sight, this makes the representation more complex, but Quaternions offer a mathematically elegant way of interpolating between two Quaternions, called Spherical Linear Interpolation (SLERP).

Quaternion SLERP [Shoemake.1985], from here on denoted as $\oplus$ can furthermore be used to extrapolate or perform a weighted interpolation between two Quaternions, where a is the weight of each component into the interpolation (with a being a value between 0 and 1):

$$\text{Quaternion}_{Interpolated} = a \cdot \text{Quaternion}_1 \oplus (1 - a) \cdot \text{Quaternion}_2 \qquad (2.1)$$

2.3.2 Complementary Filter

A simple complementary filter as described in [Lawitzki.2012] or [Mahony.2008] can already deliver very good results. A low-pass filter smooths jittery signals by averaging over a number of measurements. The bigger this set, the smoother the signal but at the cost of higher latency. It is used for processing data from the accelerometer and the compass. A high-pass filter on the other hand works like a gate that only lets through a value if it has changed enough compared to its previous value. Since gyroscopes only measure velocities, they require an integration-stage to deliver an orientation. During this integration, noise is transformed into drift which can be eliminated with a high-pass filter. Figure 2.10 shows the structure of a complementary filter that integrates data from accelerometer, compass and gyroscope to obtain a drift-free absolute orientation estimation that should still have a good dynamic response[14].

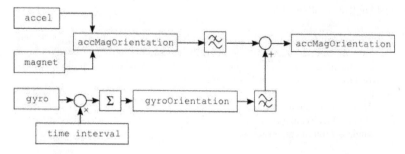

Figure 2.10: Sensor fusion with a complementary filter [Lawitzki.2012].

---

[14]Figures 2.10 and 2.11 by Paul Lawitzki. Taken from http://www.thousand-thoughts.com/2012/03/android-sensor-fusion-tutorial/

Figure 2.11 illustrates the ideal behaviour of the filters and their effects on the signal.

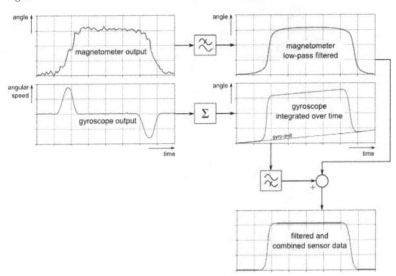

Figure 2.11: Ideal behaviour of a complementary filter [Lawitzki.2012].

2.3.3 Kalman Filter

A much better but more sophisticated solution than a simple complementary filter is a Kalman filter. The properties and power of Kalman filters are well known [Welch.2006] and have been successfully applied to numerous systems that fuse visual information with other sensor data obtained from GPS or IMU [Randeniya.2008], [Klein.2004], [Schall.2009], [Wang.2009] or simply to improve visual tracking [Weng.2006]. [Bradski.2008] and [Bleser.2009] note, that a Kalman filter is the most widely used estimator.

Kalman filter are used to address the general problem of state estimation of a discrete-time controlled process [Welch.2006]. It requires some assumptions regarding the process like a normal distribution of the noise. The main idea behind a Kalman filter is that it uses a feedback-loop between predicting the future state of the modelled system and updating it with the measured values.

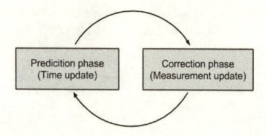

Figure 2.12: Two phases of estimator cycle as used for Kalman filter

Now both, the prediction and the update can contain uncertainty which is modelled into the generally known Kalman equations:

$$x_k = F \cdot x_{k-1} + B \cdot u_k + w_k \tag{2.2}$$

$$z_k = H_k \cdot x_k + v_k \tag{2.3}$$

x_k denotes the current n-dimensional state vector of the system. F is the n-by-n transfer matrix that connects the previous system state vector x_{k-1} with the other inputs. The n-by-c dimensional matrix B relates the control input vector u_k, which is a c-dimensional vector to the state change and finally w_k that represents the process noise. This equation is used for predicting x_k from the previous state x_{k-1}. z_k denotes the m-dimensional measurement update, where H_k specifies the relation between the measured values of z_k to the state vector x_k in form of a m-by-n matrix. Finally v_k which models the measurement noise.

Both noise variables require the following assumptions of normal distribution: $p(w) \sim N(0, Q)$, $p(v) \sim N(0, R)$ with covariances Q and R that might change with each step. By specifically using the Kalman equations, one can model dynamic motion (static model), a controlled motion (where the dynamics change according to a certain control input) or a random motion (where the motion can not be predicted well, which is modelled into the noise covariances Q and R that increase over time and therefore contain a higher uncertainty).

An increasing popular alternative to a Kalman filter is a particle filter as used in [Klein.2006], [Schon.2007] and [Choi.2012]. It allows to model elements of non-linearity and non-Gaussianity like in an extended Kalman filter by representing probability densities as a mass of points (particles) in a sequential Monte Carlo method [Arulampalam.2002].

2.4 Computer Vision

Computer Vision (CV) is the technique of allowing the computer to see. And not just to see a single picture in a video stream but also to identify and track objects, recognise patterns or determine complex structures. In the simplest case an artificial marker as in figure 2.13 is extracted from the image and the relative pose to it estimated. But also objects without markers can be tracked, which is generally known as *natural feature tracking*.

Figure 2.13: A simple artificial marker as used by the ARToolkit [Kato.1999] that consists of a thick solid black border that can easily be tracked in the camera image and an infill that can contain arbitrary content.

2.4.1 Image pyramids

As cameras get better and better, the resolution of images is increasing as well. On the one hand this is good, because more details can be captured, on the other hand it means that algorithms have to process bigger inputs which directly affects the runtime. To increase the performance of CV algorithms, images are scaled down in powers of two by means of smoothing and sub-sampling. Multiple versions of the same image at different scales are called an *image pyramid* because each image gets smaller, so the visual representation looks like a pyramid. Now the algorithm starts on the smallest image and subsequently refines the results onto higher levels of the pyramid until it reaches the original image.

2.4.2 Computer Vision Tracking

The way computers can achieve complex tracking tasks, is by breaking down the process of visual perception into smaller pieces that can be controlled and solved fast enough. The input for computer vision is usually an image captured by a camera or a video, which can be seen as a sequence of images. A solution for a problem on images can therefore be propagated onto videos. One central objective in Computer Vision is to identify and track objects or the camera motion through multiple images (called *frames*), referred to as *optical flow*. In theory every single point of two consecutive images could be compared with each other to track the camera transition. This procedure would be called *dense optical flow* which can be solved for example with the Horn and Schunck algorithm and associates a velocity with every pixel in an image. Due to its extremely high computational complexity, it is barely relevant for anything but academic purposes [Bradski.2008]. Instead, only small parts of an image, called *patches* (typically small pixel squares) are extracted and tracked. As opposed to dense optical flow, this approach is called *sparse optical flow*. It can be solved for example with the Lucas-Kanade algorithm [Lucas.1981] that rests on three assumptions [Bradski.2008, S. 324]:

- **Brightness constancy**: It assumes that the brightness of a pixel does not change from frame to frame.

- **Temporal persistence**: It assumes that the motion of a surface patch changes slowly in time which means that the temporal increments are fast enough compared to the scale of motion, so that tracked objects do not move much between two frames. If faster motion needs to be tracked, OpenCV also provides a Lucas-Kanade-implementation that works in the scale-space (on image pyramids) to be able to track faster motions.

- **Spatial coherence**: Neighbouring points in a scene belong to the same surface, have a similar motion, and project to nearby points on the image plane.

Figure 2.14 demonstrates the results of optical flow on a smartphone while walking along a corridor. Red circles are indicating the tracked points while the lines show where the corresponding point was in the previous frame. Optical flow in OpenCV is usually achieved by extracting features with the Shi-Tomasi Good-Features-To-Track-method [Shi.1994] for two consecutive frames and calculating a sparse optical flow with the Lucas-Kanade method. It is therefore often called Kanade-Lucas-Tomasi (KLT) tracker.

Finding proper regions for sparse optical flow in an image is the the first step of a tracking algorithm and the purpose of a *feature detector*. These regions are generally known as *interesting points* or *feature points* in an image, and can refer to edges, corners, blobs or other structures that have good properties, namely being easy to spot in an image and therefore robustly reproducible, even under image transformations such as rotations or scaling. A good feature detector is very fast while delivering a sufficient number of features (which can vary from hundreds to thousands). Figure 2.15 illustrates the result of the feature detection algorithm Speeded-Up robust features (SURF) by [Bay.2006] on a grey-scale image. Feature points are located in the centre of each green circle and oriented into one direction

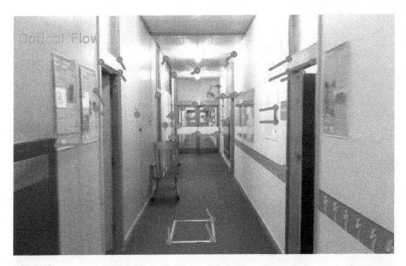

Figure 2.14: Optical Flow on a smartphone. Red circles are tracked points and red lines represent their velocity from the previous frame.

as indicated by the line going to the centre from each circle. The size of the circle represents importance. The bigger the circle, the more prominent the feature.

Once feature points are detected, they need to be compared with each other. Naive methods like cross-correlation can be used for that, or patches are transformed into a more efficient representation called *feature descriptors*. When transformed into the descriptor-representation, they can efficiently be matched with each other plus gaining robustness to illumination changes, scaling and transformations.

Finally, after matching the feature descriptors one can use the set of point-correspondences to calculated a homography that defines the projective transformation between two frames. To obtain rotational and translational information (how the camera has moved), an 8-Point algorithm can be used [Randeniya.2008, S. 114–115] that requires at least 8 point-correspondences in consecutive frames. To compensate for wrong correspondences, a Random Sample Consensus (RANSAC) algorithm discriminates the correspondences into a consensus set (inliers) that are used for the homography and outliers that are discarded.

Figure 2.16 shows the result of a full tracking-step. Features in both images were detected, described and matched. The set of correspondences was then used to estimate the homography which is marked as green rectangle.

It should be mentioned that optical flow does not contain any pattern-recognition. If a pattern should be recognised in the image (e.g. a marker), this is usually done by calculating feature descriptors and matching them against a database of saved feature descriptors. This process is very expensive (especially when using

Figure 2.15: Interest points that were detected by the feature detection algorithm SURF.

Figure 2.16: Matched features and estimated homography (green rectangle)

high-dimensional feature descriptors such as 128-dimensional Scale Invariant Feature Transform (SIFT) descriptors [Skrypnyk.2004]). The idea therefore of many marker-based AR systems is to find patterns (called *registration*) only once to recognise the marker and start an optical flow tracking from that moment on. The registration is only repeated, if the tracking fails, e.g. due to fast movement, image blur or occlusion.

2.4.3 3D reconstruction

When reconstructing the 3D environment from a series of picture from different viewpoints, bundle adjustment is often used. It has the objective to simultaneously optimise the 3D points from image projections (the 2-dimensional pictures of the real 3D world) to find the correspondences between the images, the motion of the camera and the optical characteristics of the camera taking the photography. It is the main enabling technique for Simultaneous Localisation and mapping (SLAM) systems that reconstruct an unknown environment while tracking the user motion at the same time. Individual points might not be recognised very precisely but if there are more than 10.000 points available, the systems relies on the bundle adjustment to find enough inliers to calculate a correct pose estimation.

SLAM comes in a variety of different flavours: With a mono [Davison.2007] or stereo ocular [Lemaire.2007], laser-scanners [Steux.2010], depth cameras [Pinies.2007], aided with IMU [Kleinert.2012] and even on mobile phones [Klein.2009b]. Parallel tracking and mapping (PTAM) [Klein.2007] and Dense Tracking and Mapping (DTAM) [Newcombe.2011] are similar techniques and can be subsumed as SLAM, although they work slightly different.

The main issues with SLAM-like techniques are:

- SLAM as itself is computationally very expensive. As a consequence, the tracking is usually detached from the reconstruction. While the tracking happens every frame, the (more expensive) update of the 3D map happens only in key-frames (e.g. once every two seconds).

- Many SLAM-systems require a specialised initialisation step from the user (a translation, without rotation) which can easily be done wrong. Future systems might aim to exploit pure rotational information as well [Pirchheim.2013] but current systems rely on translational information.

- Most systems assume a static environment ([Davison.2007], [Klein.2009b] and [Newcombe.2011]). Tracking will therefore fail, if the reconstructed scene changes rapidly. Newer systems like [Tan.2013] are designed for dynamic environments by allowing the 3D map to be updated and certain points to be removed.

2.4.4 Tools

For running computer-vision algorithms on mobile devices, special care has to be taken to achieve real-time performance. Since this task is very complex and requires a lot of effort, existing libraries should be used, that provide ready-to-use algorithms with highly optimised implementations and run on almost any platform. The two most extensive libraries up to date are FastCV[15] by Qualcomm and OpenCV[16]. Both libraries offer basic CV functionality such as image transformations and matrix operations and more sophisticated features such as object tracking, feature detection or 3D reconstruction. Although FastCV offers a wide range of functionality, OpenCV is much more comprehensive and has implementations of the very latest algorithms, since it is an open-source project and everyone can contribute to the source base.

A modern C++ library that enables the development of real-time 3D-reconstruction applications is the PointCloud-Library[17]. This library provides means of efficiently creating and processing 2D/3D point clouds [Rusu.2011]. It has been ported to all major platforms (Windows, Linux, Mac, Android, iOS) and is freely available under the BSD license for commercial and research use.

An entire collection of free SLAM-implementations can be found at http://openslam.org/. Mostly implemented in C++ or MatLab, these libraries serve different purposes, starting with monocular SLAM with minimalistic implementations in less than 200 lines of C-Code to general frameworks. However, none of them is particularly designed to run on mobile devices and the computational power required for some, prohibit their use on mobile devices.

2.5 Fusion of visual and inertial sensors

When actually breaking down the idea of fusing visual and inertial sensors, two fundamentally different approaches exist that have strengths and limitations respectively:

- **Loose coupling**: The visual sensor delivers an estimation of rotation and translation, so does the IMU. A Kalman filter is then used to merge those results into a meaningful output. The benefits of this approach is that both parts can be developed individually and standard algorithms for tracking like Lucas-Kanade [Lucas.1981] and 8-Point homography calculation can be used. On the other hand, the benefits that arise from the synthesis are being unused.

- **Tight coupling**: The measurements of the IMU is directly used for assisting the visual tracking by providing predictions of feature-points. The camera measurements on the other hand can be used to calibrate the IMU. Given a

---

[15]FastCV: https://developer.qualcomm.com/mobile-development/mobile-technologies/computer-vision-fastcv
[16]OpenCV: http://opencv.org
[17]PointCloud-Library: http://www.pointclouds.org

system, that has a 3D-Model of the environment (either from offline preparation or from a SLAM-like reconstruction), the measurements given from the IMU applied to the last known position of the camera can help deliver better predictions of where to search for keypoints or lines in the image, reducing the search-space dramatically.

Summarising, the difference between loose and tight coupling is whether - in loose coupling - the two tracking systems (IMU tracking and visual tracking) work independently and only their results are fused, or - in tight coupling - assist each other directly in the tracking process. The assistance in tight coupling can work in both directions: The IMU is faster than the visual tracking and can therefore provide predictions whereas the visual tracking is drift-free and can be used to calibrate the IMU to eliminate drift and remove bias.

2.5.1 Loose Coupling

[Randeniya.2008, S. 114–115] is one example of a system that uses loose coupling, by implementing the following process:

1. Perform optical flow by extracting and tracking feature points with a KLT feature tracker

2. Estimate pose from at least eight tracked non-coplanar point correspondences using the 8-Point algorithm. Only those points are being considered in the pose estimation, that are tracked for at least five consecutive frames.

Apart from Lucas-Kanade optical flow tracking, a number of detector-descriptor-based visual tracking algorithms have been proposed. [Gauglitz.2011] provides a list of different systems and their characteristics. What all these systems have in common is the need for a fast and reliable feature detection, feature description and feature matching. Chapter 6 contains an extensive evaluation of different algorithms to perform these tasks.

2.5.2 Tight Coupling

An example for tight coupling is given in [Klein.2004]. The IMU directly assists the parametric edge detector by predicting the position of the 3D model for the next camera frame. As described previously, this is only possible because the scene that should be tracked is known before and Computer Aided Design (CAD) models are available. If no CAD model exists or tracking should work in a dynamic environment, Simultaneous Localisation and Mapping (SLAM) is the approach of choice, because it can cope with an unknown, unprepared environment. On the fly, a 3D map of the scene is reconstructed and simultaneously used to track the camera motion.

Ideally a tight coupling approach would fuse SLAM that can cope with dynamic environments and pure rotations with the IMU to assist the visual tracking of the reconstructed map. However, such systems are currently not feasible to run on mobile devices unless heavily optimised.

2.6 Challenges

This section describes the typical challenges that one encounters when using hardware sensors that are built into smartphones and tablets to implement an AR system:

- **Motion blur**: Motion Blur is a smearing effect in photography that pays its toll due to the fact that cameras can not take a picture instantly but have a certain shutter speed to capture an image. Motion Blur can be caused either by rapid motion of an object or long exposure of the camera.

Figure 2.17: Steady camera (left) vs. rotating camera (right) during exposure causing motion blur.

Motion blur is often considered an impediment to visual tracking, that must be dealt with by special means. However, motion blur can contain visual cues that can be used in computer tracking systems to gain information on the motion of the camera [Klein.2009]. Later work by [Klein.2009b] not only deals with motion blur, but even exploits it as a gyroscope (to extract rotational information), that the iPhone 3G physically lacked.

- **Rolling Shutter**: Rolling-Shutter is an image acquisition method where different parts of an image are captured by scanning across the frame rather than at a single point of time. That means, not all parts of the image are recorded at exactly the same time. The advantage of such a method is that the exposure of the light capturing sensor and the readout to the memory are overlapping, hence allowing a full frame exposure without affecting the framerate [AitAider.2006, S. 58]. On the other hand, this can lead to a variety of distortions such as wobble, skew, smear or partial exposure, see figure 2.18[18]. Basically all cameras that are available in todays smartphones and tablets use a rolling shutter. As with motion blur, the rolling shutter effect can be addressed in three different ways: it can be ignored (which is acceptable if the camera is not undergoing fast motion or if only static objects are observed),

---

[18]Rolling Shutter Image: http://commons.wikimedia.org/wiki/File:CMOS_rolling_shutter_distortion.jpg, CC ShareAlike license: http://creativecommons.org/licenses/by-sa/3.0/deed.en

one can try to compensate for it as in [Klein.2009b], or even expose it to directly measure velocity from a single image, given a fast enough high-resolution camera, small accelerations and known models [AitAider.2006].

Figure 2.18: Rolling Shutter Effect (By Axel1963 via Wikimedia Commons)

- **Sensor drift** (for IMU): The inertial sensors gyroscope and accelerometer can be used to measure changes in the orientation and position. They are well suited for capturing short, possibly fast movements but create a cumulated error called sensor drift over time [Schall.2009], [Randeniya.2008]. This happens because those sensors can only measure differences in the orientation or position and not absolute values, so the output is calculated by integrating those changes over a certain period of time. The process of determining the position of an object starting from a known position and advancing it based on estimated speeds over time is known as *dead reckoning*. It is used for example in car navigation to overcome GPS outtakes but when relying on IMU data only, the result can contain an unbounded position error [Bleser.2009, S. 59].

Figure 2.19 and figure 2.20 visualise the effects of sensor drift when single- and double-integrating noisy data.

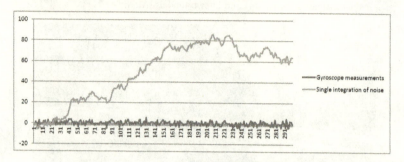

Figure 2.19: Visualisation of sensor drift if gyroscope data that contains random-noise is single-integrated. 300 data-points correspond to approx. 10 seconds without correction.

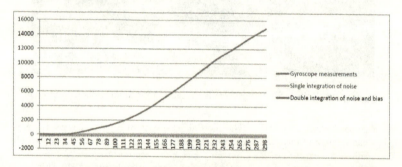

Figure 2.20: Visualisation of sensor drift if gyroscope data that contains random-noise is double-integrated (as used in dead reckoning). Red and green lines are the same as in figure 2.19

Figure 2.21 shows two screenshots from the CityViewAR application, that were taken without undergoing camera movement (as can be seen from the background), but since the application only uses IMU data, the accumulated rotation error becomes visible as the rendered building has "floated" to the left.

Figure 2.21: CityViewAR application that suffers from sensor drift.

- **Sensor precision and outtakes** (for GPS): The Global Positioning System (GPS) is by its design currently limited to a maximal precision of about 5m for civil purposes. This can be increased significantly by using Differential Global Positioning System (DGPS), modern Global Navigation Satellite System (GNSS) receivers (that combine two standards, GPS and GLONASS[19]) or Real Time Kinematic (RTK) satellite navigation that uses multiple base-stations to achieve even centimetre accuracy[20]. But in reality, smartphones only have a single GPS receiver that is always affected by noise and is only available, if the satellite signal is strong enough, which is not the case if travelling in a tunnel or in buildings, for example. A system that relies on GPS must therefore cope with outtakes and noisy measurements. [Randeniya.2008] suggests to fuse measurements from an IMU with visual sensors to overcome outtakes while performing road-navigation. If only the GPS is used for global positioning in an AR system without any filtering, the augmented objects will constantly jump to a new location on each update even though the user might not have moved at all, see figure 2.22.

Newer DGPS/RTK systems like the Piksi[21] by Swift Navigation[22] are promising devices to improve GPS precision up to centimetre-accuracy in the future. Similar devices might be built into smartphones and tablet PCs one day.

---

[19]Globalnaja nawigazionnaja sputnikowaja sistema (rus.) (GLONASS)
[20]RTK-Receiver by North-Surveying: http://www.northsurveying.com/index.php/gps-rtk-receivers
[21]Piksi on Kickstarter: http://www.kickstarter.com/projects/swiftnav/piksi-the-rtk-gps-receiver
[22]Swift-Navigation: http://docs.swift-nav.com/wiki/Main_Page

Figure 2.22: CityViewAR application that suffers from "jumping buildings" whenever a GPS update is received.

3 Related Work

3.1 Augmented Reality on Mobile Devices

Mobile devices such as smartphones and tablet PCs have become increasingly popular due to the fact that they provide sufficient computational power for many tasks. And with the increasing number of available apps, the range of applications for smartphones seems almost unlimited (starting from guiding blind people[1] to teaching anatomy[2] or enhancing the drawing experience of simple colour drawings[3]). Additionally, many phones offer a variety of sensors, built directly into the device, such as a gyroscope, an accelerometer a magnetic compass, GPS receiver and a camera. Combined with the touch-interface smartphones offer an intuitive user-interface, often referred to as *natural user-interface*.

In terms of components of an AR system, smartphones combine all four parts into a single device: Users interact by pointing the device and touching the screen that displays the augmented reality in a video see-through way. The device also can be used to track the user with the sensors available and finally it offers enough computational power to enable a real-time AR experience. Smartphones also offer a significantly more accepted form-factor compared to heavy head-mounted displays as for example used in Archeoguide [Vlahakis.2002], see figure 3.1.

Companies as Metaio[4] or Layar[5] have evolved entirely from the field of augmented reality. They provide frameworks for developing AR applications on mobile devices (Software Development Kit (SDK)), namely Metaio SDK and Layar SDK respectively. Both SDKs offer marker-based visual tracking, natural feature tracking (sometimes referred to as *markerless tracking*), GPS tracking and tracking with inertial sensors such as the gyroscope, the accelerometer and the compass. The SDKs are available for mobile devices running Android, iOS and Unity[6] [7] [8].

Another company is Qualcomm[9], a chipset manufacturer who is developing a

---

[1]List of apps for blind or visual impaired people: http://www.applevis.com/apps/ios-apps-for-blind-and-vision-impaired

[2]Anatomy & Physiology Revealed: https://itunes.apple.com/app/id510182642

[3]ColAR Mix app: http://colarapp.com/

[4]Metaio: http://www.metaio.com

[5]Layar: https://www.layar.com

[6]Layar tracking capabilities: https://www.layar.com/products/app/

[7]Metaio tracking capabilities: http://dev.metaio.com/sdk/tracking-config/

[8]Layar FAQs: http://www.layar.com/documentation/browser/howtos/layar-vision-doc/layar-vision-faqs/

[9]Qualcomm: http://www.qualcomm.com/

Figure 3.1: System setup as used in Archeoguide [Vlahakis.2002] for mobile Augmented Reality

mobile AR framework called Vuforia[10]. The Vuforia SDK similar to the previous two frameworks offers marker-based tracking as well as natural feature tracking on Android, iOS and Unity[11] but no tracking with IMU. In contrast to the previously mentioned companies, Qualcomm also develops a computer vision library (FastCV [12]) and mobile processors built into new generation smartphones[13].

Yet another SDK, implementing natural feature tracking is the Pointcloud SDK[14]. Compared to the other SDKs mentioned before, it only supports iOS (Data as of December 2013). Finally, the *Mobile AR Framework*[15] from the HitLab NZ needs to be mentioned, because the solution approach from this thesis was built into it. Currently it supports only outdoor IMU tracking with GPS positioning and is limited to the Android platform.

Recent developments show that SLAM approaches, where the 3D environment is mapped and tracked at the same time are not only feasible on mobile devices but also offer remarkable results [Klein.2009b]. Hence, the Metaio SDK recently added a SLAM implementation they call *Instant Mapping*[16], Pointcloud promotes their SDK by offering 3D tracking and mapping and Qualcomm is actively developing a similar solution (as displayed at the ISMAR 2012[17] and ISMAR 2013)

To sum it up, most mobile AR systems are based on IMU tracking or visual tracking (either with markers or natural features). But in the future, mobile devices might be able to map and track the environment in real-time. However, as until today, no system has been published that performs tightly coupled sensor fusion on a mobile device that unifies SLAM with IMU tracking. Metaio is using multiple sensors only to smooth the result or combine multiple markers to improve tracking[18]. And although visual-only systems are becoming more robust, they simply do not exploit all available sensors of modern smartphones and tablets, thus being a lot more computationally expensive and error-prone to certain problems as described in chapter 2.6.

---

[10]Qualcomm Vuforia: http://www.qualcomm.com/solutions/augmented-reality
[11]Vuforia capabilities: https://developer.vuforia.com/resources/sample-apps
[12]FastCV: https://developer.qualcomm.com/mobile-development/mobile-technologies/computer-vision-fastcv
[13]Snapdragon processor: https://developer.qualcomm.com/discover/chipsets-and-modems/snapdragon
[14]Pointcloud SDK: http://pointcloud.io/
[15]Mobile AR Framework: http://www.hitlabnz.org/index.php/products/mobile-ar-framework
[16]Metaio Instant Mapping: https://dev.metaio.com/toolbox/instant-mapping/
[17]SLAM on a mobile device by Qualcomm: http://www.youtube.com/watch?v=T70hgNvpUxE
[18]Metaio sensor fusion capabilities: http://dev.metaio.com/sdk/tracking-configuration/fuser/

3.2 Visual-only Mobile AR Systems

A lot of AR systems have been published so far, even on mobile phones. But most of the systems running on mobile phones are only able to track markers. Only recent advances made it possible to achieve a full 6-DOF pose tracking on mobile phones. In this chapter I want to take a closer look at systems that perform tracking only with a camera.

There are many more systems that already achieve accurate real-time localisation from tracking natural features, often by using known 3D-models of the target scene, such as in [Jiang.2004], [Comport.2006] or [Tamaazousti.2011], but these systems are computationally too expensive and cannot run on a mobile device or require tedious creation of 3D models before they can be used.

3.2.1 Mobile Pose Tracking from Natural Features in real-time

One successful approach in 2008 was done by [Wagner.2008]. Their system is able to achieve real-time (up to 20Hz) pose tracking from natural features on mobile phones by using heavily modified feature descriptors, namely SIFT [Lowe.2004] and Ferns [Ozuysal.2007]. They dramatically speeded up the SIFT descriptor by replacing the originally proposed Difference-of-Gaussians keypoint detector with the Features from Accelerated Segment Test (FAST) [Rosten.2010] corner detector and combining two complementary methods (SIFT and Ferns) that share the common parts, as can be seen in figure 3.2.

The two pipelines share the FAST corner detector (top box in figure 3.2) to detect feature points in the camera image and a Gauss-Newton iteration to refine camera pose, originally estimated from a homography (bottom box). The feature detector is dynamically adjusted to yield approximately 150 features per frame which they found to be a good compromise between getting enough features for matching and processing speed. [Wagner.2008, S. 127]

To further speed up tracking performance on mobile devices, 8x8 image patches that are blurred with a 3x3 Gaussian kernel are matched with a Sum of Absolute Differences (SAD) similarity score. Additionally they had the constraint of tracking features only in a 25px search radius. For a fast search of neighbouring features, all new coordinates are entered into a 2D grid which allows to perform search in almost constant time per frame. To perform the actual matching, Spill Trees (a variation of k-d Trees) were used.

Their system is tracking "good" and "bad" features, where "good" refers to features that passed outlier-tests and were considered in the pose-estimation, while "bad" points were filtered in that step, resulting in a significant speed up since there was no need to describe and match bad points against the SIFT database again.

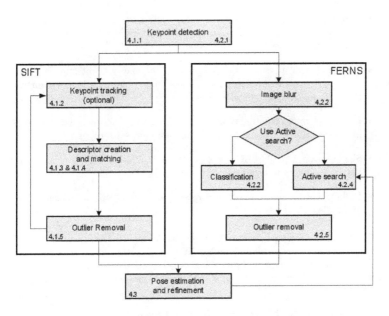

Figure 3.2: Pipeline of pose tracking system on mobile phones by [Wagner.2008].

3.2.2 Parallel Tracking and Mapping on Mobile Phones

In [Klein.2009b] the authors ported their already existing SLAM-like system named PTAM from [Klein.2007] to the Apple iPhone 3G. In contrast to previously described methods, this was the first published system that achieved simultaneous localisation and mapping on a mobile phone.

They used the following adaptations in order to make PTAM feasible on a smart-phone:

- Images are received at a resolution of only 240x320 pixels.

- Good-Features-to-Track keypoints ([Shi.1994]) have to appear on image pyramid levels L0 (240x320), L1 (120x160) and L2 (60x80); the exhaustive search starts at the L2 image and is propagated to L0.

- The number of measurements per point in the map and the number of keyframes is actively reduced by removing redundant points and frames to improve the performance of the bundle adjustment.

- Full-frame rotation estimation (replacing a gyroscope, that the iPhone 3G physically lacks) is used to deal with motion blur.

- Single expensive RANSAC homography fit is replaced with an incremental update (common in incremental monocular SLAM)

- Rolling shutter compensation is done with a constant velocity model, outside of bundle adjustment.

The authors' conclusion is that keyframe-based SLAM can operate on mobile phones. In comparison to the PC implementation, they showed the limitations and also note that future generation smartphones will be shipped with more capabilities like gyroscopes, which can be exploited to improve tracking.

3.3 IMU-only Mobile AR Systems

Most of the AR frameworks mentioned earlier either have a IMU tracking configuration, like Metaio SDK or are entirely based on IMU tracking, like HitLab NZ's Mobile AR Framework. For outdoor tracking, all these systems additionally require GPS sensors to obtain the global position of the user (latitude and longitude).

Furthermore there are numerous more applications that entirely rely on IMU sensors, like a 3D AR Compass[19] or the open-source Augmented Reality engine mixare[20] that fuses compass, accelerometer and sometimes gyroscope to obtain an absolute orientation of the device. Simple filters are often used to smooth the results.

---

[19]3D AR Compass: https://github.com/ratana/rotation-vector-compass
[20]Mixare Open-Source AR framework: http://www.mixare.org

3.4 Hybrid systems

The following systems use a fusing strategy to combine visual tracking with IMU sensors in order to improve the tracking performance and to overcome the problems described in 2.6. They were selected because they represent a milestone in recent research or the current state-of-the-art.

3.4.1 Model-based Visio-Inerial Tracking

[Klein.2004] developed in 2004 a tightly coupled system that used a gyroscope mounted onto a camera (see figure 3.3) to overcome the limitations of one another. It fuses measurements from both sensors in a statistical Kalman filter and uses the gyroscope to assist the parametric edge-detection.

Figure 3.3: Rate gyroscopes affixed to a camera, as used by [Klein.2004].

Visual tracking is used to fit a predicted 3D CAD-model to a real model, captured by the camera by means of edge-detection and a local search to correct errors between the prediction and the capture. For fast movements this system fails, since motion-blur pollutes the data and no edges can be detected. At this point, the gyroscope data was used to overcome this limitation, since it yields precise data when moving fast, but incorporates drift when standing still. Their strategy is shown in figure 3.4. The bottom box contains the Kalman filter that estimates the system state. What clearly can be seen in this diagram is that translations can not be measured with a gyroscope, so the visual sensor can not fall back on inertial sensors for fast translations but only for fast rotations.

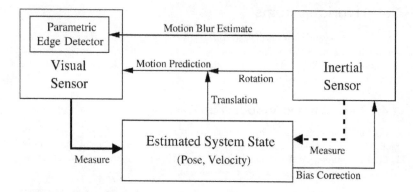

Figure 3.4: Tight coupling strategy for fusing a gyroscope with visual sensors to achieve robust tracking as used in [Klein.2004, S.770].

Their system had a number of severe limitations:

- The inertial sensor was only able to measure rotational velocity. Linear velocity was estimated from visual measurements [Klein.2004, S.773].

- The system depends on data prepared off-line such as 3D CAD-models for the tracked object, which limits its use to scenes, where actual models exist [Klein.2004, S.775].

- Their system had no registration stage, so registration had to be done manually with no graceful recovery from tracking failure [Klein.2004, S.775].

- Tracking of (rapidly) moving objects is not supported at all [Klein.2004, S.775].

In [Bleser.2009] the authors give an overview of different systems that perform sensor fusion and the effects of fully exploiting accelerometer in the fusion process. They furthermore introduce a new device that joins an XSens MT9-C IMU with a monochrome PGR camera in a single box, they named CamIMU (see figure 3.5) that is significantly smaller than the hardware used by [Klein.2004]. The XSens IMU delivers measured angular velocity, accelerations and also absolute orientation. Their tightly coupled visual tracking systems starts with a manually entered initial position and uses a simplified textured CAD model of the environment in conjunction with an advanced Lucas-Kanade feature tracker. They refer to this technique as analysis-by-synthesis. Visual measurement updates are obtained by as least four 2D/3D correspondences and fused with IMU updates in an extended Kalman filter.

As noted by the authors, the model generation and maintenance is tedious and the assumption of a static environment is often violated, therefore the system should be extended with real-time SLAM capabilities.

Figure 3.5: Miniaturisation of devices that combine IMU and a camera in a single device (CamIMU, as used by [Bleser.2009]).

3.4.2 IMU Sensor fusion with Visual Panorama Tracker

The system proposed in [Schall.2009] uses a huge number of different sensors loosely coupled and built into a handheld device (see figure 3.6). It fuses data obtained from the GPS and inertial sensors with visual tracking to correct the initial pose estimation and compensate for sensor drift. Additionally a thermometer, barometer and a GPRS-modem are used to improve position and attitude estimates.

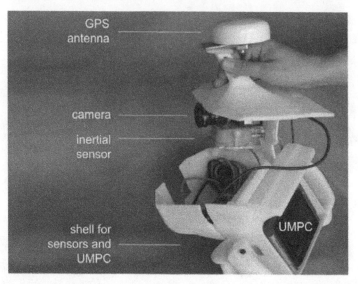

Figure 3.6: Handheld device used by [Schall.2009] to track the users' global pose

In comparison to other systems, no artificial markers or models are required because their visual sensor uses a panorama tracking technique that online creates a map of features from the environment to track orientations. Even if occlusions occur (e.g. if a car crosses the field of view) the system is able to re-initialise and continue tracking from that map. The visual tracker uses a similar approach as SLAM with the difference that it creates a flat, dense map which is not updated once it is created. 2D-2D point correspondences between the environment map and the camera image are matched using a FAST corner detector and normalized cross correlation between warped 8x8 pixel patches and the input image which has a resolution of 320x240 pixels.

Their system has the following four subsystems for the actual fusion (figure 3.7):

- **Position Kalman filter** that fuses a barometer with a DGPS/RTK receiver as well as position correction from the Austrian Positioning Service to achieve sub-meter accuracy. The output is a global position in the Universal Transverse Mercator (UTM) format which will be used directly in the final output.

- **Attitude Kalman filter** that fuses Accelerometer, Magnetometer and Gyroscope to deliver rolling, pitching and yawing.

- **Panorama Tracker** that uses the camera and the motion model of the inertial tracker to provide more accurate priors under fast motions. This tracker also delivers roll, pitch and yaw.

- **Orientation Finite State Machine** that fuses the Attitude Kalman filter and the Panorama tracker in such a way that it takes under consideration if the visual tracker deviates from the inertial tracker. If so, depending on whether visual tracking is valid (number of features detected > 20) or not it uses the most trustworthy tracker. The output of the state machine is delivered as result.

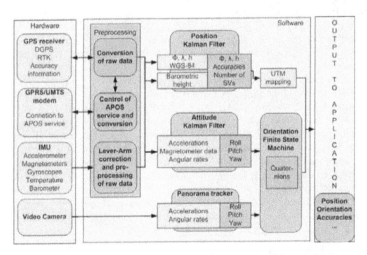

Figure 3.7: Overview of the system proposed by [Schall.2009]

The only downside of this system is that it requires special hardware that is usually not available in todays smartphones. The authors also suggest to tightly couple the GPS with the IMU and to extend the visual tracker to take kinematic movements into account.

3.4.3 Multi-camera Sensor fusion

In [Randeniya.2008] the authors present a system that loosely fuses visual and inertial sensors for land navigation. When navigating a car, GPS is frequently used to determine the current position. But this approach suffers from potential outages (e.g. when driving in a tunnel). The idea behind their system is to overcome those outages by using inertial sensors and supplementing them with visual sensors to compensate for sensor drift.

Their setup uses a car that is equipped with the following sensors

- Two monocular cameras, one facing to the front, one to the side

- Navigational grade IMU

- Two GPS receivers

When driving a car, the environment is highly dynamic, so offline prepared models can not be used. Instead, natural feature tracking with a KLT feature tracker is used. If a feature is tracked in at least five consecutive frames, it is used as input to the eight-point algorithm (as first described by [LonguetHiggins.1987]) for estimating the rotation and translation [Randeniya.2008, S.114]. For the sensor fusion, a linear error-model was assumed, which allows to use a Kalman filter for the fusion. One local Kalman filter is used only for the visual sensor and a Master Kalman filter was used for joining the results from the visual sensor with the IMU data. In contrast to [Klein.2004], this system uses the inertial sensors for estimating rotation and translation.

In [Oskiper.2013] a sophisticated AR system is presented that tightly fuses IMU with GPS and two cameras in an extended Kalman filter (see fig. 3.8) to provide jitter-free, robust, real-time 6-DOF tracking built into binoculars.

The wide field-of-view camera (fig. 3.8 bottom left) is used in combination with the gyroscope for a 6-DOF tracking that is refined with the rotational information obtained from the narrow field-of-view camera (fig. 3.8 bottom right) to eliminate jittering and for augmentation. Additionally visual landmark matching and panorama tracking mechanisms enable the device for rapid global correction of orientation.

What prohibits this system to run on a modern smartphone is the specialised hardware that is required. Some smartphones are equipped with two cameras, but usually one is front-faced and one is back-faced.

3.5 Hybrid Systems on Mobile Phones

No hybrid system for a mobile device has been published so far, that makes use of all the sensors that could potentially contribute to the tracking. [Oskiper.2013] clearly points out why sensor fusion has not found wide application yet on smartphones, despite the availability of gyroscopes and accelerometers: the quality of these sensors is poor and the synchronisation with the camera a non-trivial task.

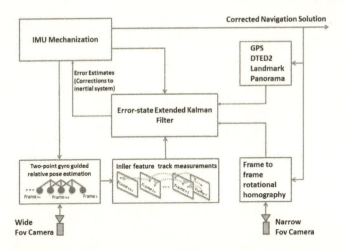

Figure 3.8: System diagram of Augmented Reality Binoculars from [Oskiper.2013]

Rare examples of hybrid systems on mobile devices is the Metaio SDK, that uses sensor fusion only to smooth visual tracking with IMU measurements or to compensate for a short tracking failure of the visual sensor; another example is [Kurz.2011] where the IMU is used to determine gravity and improve the visual rendering of objects (e.g. flame of candles, see figure 3.9).

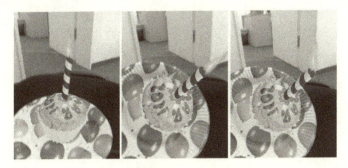

Figure 3.9: Mobile Augmented Reality that is gravity-aware and renders the light of a candle accordingly [Kurz.2011].

4 Use-Case

This chapter describes cultural heritage as a use-case for Augmented Reality by showing the benefits, existing systems and finally the newly developed application Goldfields Explorer which can be used to experience reconstructions of two buildings when visiting the Otago goldfields in New Zealand.

4.1 Augmented Reality for Cultural Heritage

Augmented Reality has a wide field of applications, starting from navigational information [Dunser.2012] to surgical assistance systems where information that would otherwise be invisible to the surgeon [Klein.2009, S. 1] could be superimposed on the patient. For this thesis, the field of cultural heritage was chosen, because the underlying AR framework was originally designed for this purpose. Furthermore, cultural heritage is an important field of research, but the huge effort of researchers is frequently bundled in a thesis or scientific papers that are not easily accessible to a wider audience. Especially tourists and hobby archaeologists often do not have access to these resources, especially when on-site. But the rapid distribution and popularity of smartphones and tablet PCs combined with the required computational power to handle mobile AR [Kounavis.2012] offers a unique chance. Many people nowadays own a smartphone or a tablet and know how to interact with it. By providing an application that runs on their private devices and delivers information directly on-site, the knowledge and experience of the researcher can easily be transferred and made accessible to a wide range of people. In enables visitors to experience a virtual tour at their fingertip [Liu.2009].

Cultural heritage applications that run on mobile devices offer a couple of benefits compared to classical information panels, books, maps and tourist guides:

- information can be provided on-site and location-based which enhances the relevance drastically

- data can be presented in an innovative, interactive and entertaining way

- the interaction is intuitive, natural and efficient in communication [Furht.2011]

- users can prepare their tour in advance and decide where to go; they can revisit the information about what they saw afterwards to learn even more

- it is cheap, since no human resource is required to operate it and no special equipment must be purchased or built - people just use their private smartphones and tablets.

- people can use the same app for multiple purposes: information and education, entertainment or navigation

- the physical structures like ruins are most likely static, so is the content

- the original site can sometimes be reconstructed and the model can be digitally superimposed on the remaining ruins

4.2 Existing AR Systems for Cultural Heritage

Already in the year 2000 a system called Archeoguide [Vlahakis.2002] was developed with the goal of a mobile AR application to provide a personalized electronic guide to outdoor archaeological sites including map-views and AR-views of reconstructed 3D-Models [Vlahakis.2002, S.52]. Archeoguide enhanced information presentation on Greece's Olympia archaeological site by means of mobile computing and Augmented Reality. To achieve this, the system required the user to wear a heavy head-mounted display and a backpack with a laptop which lead to a bad user-evaluation and low acceptance, simply because it was uncomfortable to wear. However, they already had the idea of using AR for cultural heritage and to achieve this by fusing different sensors [Vlahakis.2002, S.53]). [Fritz.2005] describes another AR system called PRISMA, that has the goal of enhancing tourism experience by providing visual augmentation. A head-mounted display that is fixed to a static structure is used as display and an IMU sensor is used for tracking the current orientation. In [Liu.2009] the authors built an Augmented Reality device for the digital reconstruction of Yuangmingyuan. Statically mounted binoculars provide an optical see-through display that is connected to a computer nearby to perform the tracking and rendering of the virtual objects. Last-mentioned, the "Augmented Reality for Basel" - challenge[1] was held as part of the ISMAR 2011 and led to a couple of commercial tourism applications for mobile phones, like a navigation app or a museum finder with a built-in audio guide.

So Augmented Reality clearly found its way into cultural heritage. [Furht.2011] has another vision and suggest a mobile system with which the user can take a picture of an artifact and the system will identify it, by comparing it with a database. Once identified, the system could provide details about the object.

In 2011 the HitLab New Zealand release an application called CityViewAR[2] [Lee.2012] with the goal of helping people to remember how the city centre looked like before the dramatic earthquakes that hit Christchurch on the 4th of September 2010 and 22nd of February 2011. The user can walk around in Christchurch and look through his hand-held smartphone at reconstructed 3D models that are superimposed onto the scene where the original buildings used to be (figure 4.1). However, this system only relies on GPS, electronic compass and accelerometer which leads to a rather unsatisfying experience, since the buildings are "floating" in the space

---

[1]AR for Basel challenge: http://www.perey.com/AugmentedRealityForBasel
[2]CityViewAR: http://www.hitlabnz.org/index.php/products/cityviewar

and are not precisely overlayed with the remainings. The CityViewAR app is using the Mobile AR Framework, developed by the HitLab and used for a variety of other apps, such as GeoBoids[3] [Lindeman.2012] (figure 4.2), AntarcticAR [Lee.2013] (figure 4.3) and the Goldfields Explorer which will be explained in the next chapter.

Figure 4.1: Screenshot of the CityViewAR application

---

[3]GeoBoids download: `https://play.google.com/store/apps/details?id=com.hitlabnz.geoboids`

Figure 4.2: Screenshot of the GeoBoids game

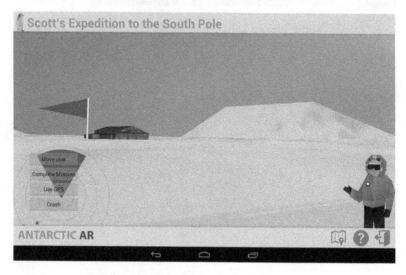

Figure 4.3: Screenshot of the AntarcticAR application

4.3 Goldfields Explorer for Bendigo

As a use-case for demonstrating the improvements described in this thesis, an Android application was developed, called Goldfields Explorer for Bendigo. The Goldfields Explorer is a virtual guide for the Bendigo gold-mining town, located in Otago, New Zealand. Bendigo was inhabited by gold-miners[4] and their families during the gold-rush that started in 1861 after Gabriel Read found gold in what now is called Gabriels Gully[5]. The application contains three parts that seamlessly fit into each other:

- An AR-view where the user can use his tablet or smartphone as video see-through display to show reconstructed 3D models directly on top of the real scene (see figure 4.4).

Figure 4.4: 3D reconstruction of the Bendigo School superimposed on the camera image in the Augmented Reality mode of the Goldfields Explorer

- A list-view where the user can select one of the prepared sites, read information about it and look at historical images such as plans, contracts or even the school rolls. Searching and sorting can be used to quickly access specific content (figure 4.5).

- A map-view where the user can find the prepared sites on a map to learn where they were located, including mines, tramway routes and water races. When using the application on-site, the user can enable position-tracking to see himself as he walks along one of the five prepared hiking-tracks (figure 4.6).

---

[4] http://www.teara.govt.nz/en/gold-and-gold-mining
[5] http://www.teara.govt.nz/en/1966/gold-discoveries/page-2

Figure 4.5: Screenshot of the list-view in the Goldfields Explorer application

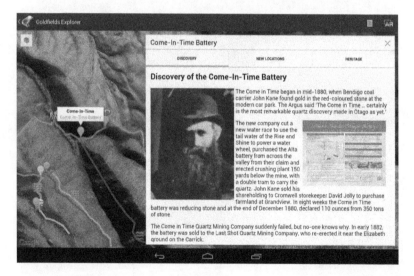

Figure 4.6: Screenshot of the map-view in the Goldfields Explorer application

The following guidelines were stated by [Wagner.2007, S. 16] and incorporated into the design while developing the application:

- **Low cost**: The application must run on off-the-shelf devices. The Goldfields Explorer is a self-contained Android application that runs on all modern smartphones and tablets; it will be available for download from the Google Play Store for free[6].

- **Robust and fool-proof**: Users run the application on their private smartphones and tablets, so they already know how to operate the hardware. The user-interface on the other hand, was designed to be as simple and minimalistic as possible. Templates and coherent graphics were used to create a consistent user-experience.

- **Self contained operation and networking support**: The Goldfields Explorer runs offline to display the information about the sites and the Augmented Reality mode. Only when entering the map-mode, a network-connection is required to load the map tiles, but once downloaded no connection is needed anymore, unless the user starts panning on the map.

- **Tracking support**: When running the application, real-time tracking takes place: the GPS position of the user is being tracked to calculate the distance to nearby sites or to show his position on the map. When switching to the AR mode, the built-in inertial sensors (accelerometer, gyroscope and compass) are used additionally to track the user's pose. For augmentation, the built-in camera is used.

- **Rapid prototyping**: The Goldfields Explorer is a standalone application and was built upon the HitLab NZ's Mobile AR Framework; it uses existing infrastructure from the framework and it can be reused for other locations by simply exchanging the content.

- **Content creation**: Many AR applications, especially research applications turn out to be so-called One-Trick-Ponies. When using it for the first time, they create a "wow-effect" that quickly wears off. After that, users demand a practical benefit from the application, which requires meaningful content. The Goldfields Explorer contains highly compressed, selected information about the Otago region and uses AR only as a medium of interaction and communication. The preparation of content is not trivial, because data is stored in HTML web pages on the device, which violates the requirement of having a user-friendly content creation pipeline. But since the content is highly static it only needs to be created once.

---

[6]Download-link for the Goldfields Explorer from the Google Play Store: https://play.google.com/store/apps/details?id=com.hitlabnz.og

4.4 Available data

The system described in this thesis has to cope with outdoor environments, without previous preparation of the scene. This means that no markers will be placed in the scene (as used by ARToolkit [Kato.1999] or [Wang.2009]) and tracking should work with natural features or without visual tracking at all. The GPS coordinates for many scenes of the Goldfields Explorer are only available as rough estimates, because the right locations often can not be determined exactly. As pointed out by [Klein.2009, S. 2], the primary challenge for AR applications is a robust and accurate registration. Still, this work does not focus on the registration by itself but only on the tracking. This results in the effect, that objects in the scene will stick to their position, but might be misaligned by a few meters due to inaccurate GPS data. For this particular use-case, such a behaviour is acceptable because the true location is not known anyway.

The target environment for the Goldfields Explorer is scrubland, a picture of a typical scene is given below.

Figure 4.7: Typical scene for the Goldfields Explorer. Wide area bush with occasional ruins.

5 Solution Approach

As pointed out in chapter 3, hybrid systems which combine a range of technologies (e.g. visual tracking with inertial sensors) present a promising solution to the main challenges of AR applications, namely the registration and the tracking. These systems can be used indoor as-well as outdoor, have a potentially high precision and are not limited by the usage-time (e.g. accelerometer measurements will drift off after some time and provide no longer meaningful data). This resulted in the decision to follow a hybrid approach to build the next generation AR system that uses different complementary methods to overcome the limitations of individual techniques.

5.1 Concept

A high-level overview of the originally intended, loosely coupled system is given in figure 5.1.

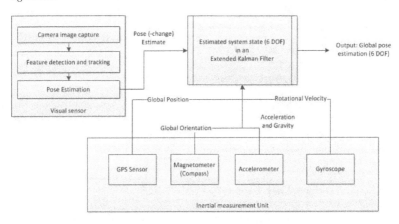

Figure 5.1: Abstract component-diagram of a hybrid 6-DOF tracking system

This diagram summarises what the individual components contribute to the global pose tracking. The GPS sensor provides the first 3-DOF tracker by supplying a global position estimation and the compass a global orientation estimation that both can be used for initialisation as well as for drift-correction. The gyroscope measures the rotational velocity and - in conjunction with the accelerometer and compass - delivers the second 3-DOF tracker to estimate the absolute orientation of the device. As a complementary system, the visual tracker captures images, tracks natural features and calculates the relative pose changes of the camera from image to image. It is therefore a second pillar, this system could rely on, but only delivers estimations of how the camera has changed and not where it currently is (in terms of a global position such as longitude and latitude). It therefore can not be used for registration.

This system design is inherently complex due to the fusion of asynchronous sensors that have different data-types, precisions and errors in a single extended Kalman filter. Details on how such an extended Kalman filter can be implemented can be found in [Klein.2004], [Schall.2009], [Bleser.2009] and [Oskiper.2013].

5.2 Target Platform

For implementing the above described concept, smartphones and tablets running the Android operating system were picked as target devices, because of the following reasons:

- Nowadays they are widely available at affordable prices.

- They have a variety of sensors which are required for the system described in this thesis.

- Developing for Android is cheaper than for iOS because there are no developer fees.

- The underlying Mobile AR framework into which this work was integrated is written in Java for Android.

Although Android was picked as target platform, the fusion approach can also be implemented and used on other platforms such as iOS and Windows Phone.

5.3 Visio-Inertial Fusion Approach

After evaluating different techniques for visual tracking (see chapter 6), the fastest and steadiest algorithms were implemented using OpenCV and evaluated on a smartphone:

- FAST [Rosten.2010] feature detector that delivers a ranked set of detected feature points. Only the 150 - 500 best feature points are considered for feature description.

- Oriented FAST and Rotated BRIEF (ORB) [Rublee.2011] and Fast Retina Keypoint (FREAK) [Alahi.2012] feature descriptors. Both are binary descriptors that can rapidly be matched with a binary XOR operation, followed by a population count.

- Brute-force matching delivers the best results simply because the number of elements that need to be matched is so small and other matching algorithms like KD-trees require the constructions of additional data-structures in each frame that are not reused and therefore generate a lot of overhead.

To validate the correspondences that have been calculated from the tracking, a homography is calculated using a RANSAC-algorithm, as described in chapter 2.4.2. Figure 5.2 shows the visual tracking while walking along the corridor. Unfortunately even with very efficient algorithms being used, no acceptable frame-rate (>10 fps) can be achieved on a Samsung Galaxy S2 using naive detector-descriptor based tracking without additional optimisation. The standard optical flow implementation is equally bad, if not even worse (<5 fps).

Figure 5.2: Detector-Descriptor-based tracking on a smartphone. Red and green circles are tracked points and their lines represent the velocity from the previous frame. Green points represent the consensus-set from the RANSAC-homography calculation.

5.4 IMU Sensor Fusion Approach

After realising that visual tracking and SLAM systems on mobile phones - if not particularly well implemented - are computationally too expensive, another approach was found that delivers extraordinary results without visual tracking. This approach is described in this chapter.

5.4.1 Android Sensor Fusion

Luckily, Android already has a Kalman filter implemented that fuses gyroscope data with measurements from the compass and the accelerometer[1]. The fusion provides virtual sensors, like a calibrated, drift-free gyroscope and an orientation sensor (called Rotation Vector) that contains an absolute orientation according to magnetic north and gravity.

The calibrated gyroscope outperforms any other sensor in terms of precision and responsiveness with the only problem, that it delivers only a relative orientation. The orientation sensor on the other hand delivers an absolute orientation but has certain problems, like a slight latency and correction, taking place even if not moving, which creates the impression of "floating objects".

5.4.2 Fusing Virtual Sensors

As indicated before, Android already provides two good virtual sensors. The novel idea is to fuse virtual sensors - that are already the result of a sensor fusion step - instead of hardware sensors to achieve even better results. The calibrated gyroscope provides a very responsive, almost drift-free measurement and the orientation sensor absolute orientation with respect to magnetic north and gravity. The fusion flow is illustrated in figure 5.3 where the Improved Orientation Sensor (right bottom box) is the main contribution of this thesis.

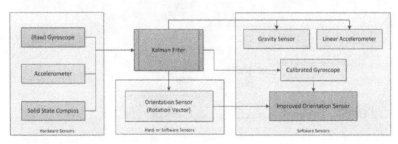

Figure 5.3: Overview of hardware and virtual sensors and how measurements flow to perform sensor fusion.

---

[1]Android Kalman filter implementation: https://android.googlesource.com/platform/frameworks/native/+/master/services/sensorservice/Fusion.cpp

The calibrated gyroscope measures changes in rotation, so these changes need to be integrated to obtain an orientation (represented as Quaternion); the orientation sensor already outputs Quaternions. So the simplest way of fusing both is to perform a Quaternion SLERP (see chapter 2.3.1):

$$\text{Improved Orientation Sensor 1} = \text{Orientation}_{Gyroscope} \cdot w \ \oplus \qquad (5.1)$$
$$\text{Orientation}_{RotationVector} \cdot (1 - w)$$

which already yielded exceptional results. Only a tiny problem remained, namely a slow floating, even if the device is at rest due to the small but constant correction of the orientation sensor. However, the floating was already dramatically reduced compared to the original orientation sensors because of the additional stabilisation of the gyroscope. This approach is preferable for most Augmented Reality applications, because it delivers a robust pose estimation but if drifted off, the user simply has to stop and wait, until the correction has taken place. The value of w should be close to 1 (e.g. 0.995).

The second novel insight that led to another approach was: "*The more you move, the more you can correct*" which is the positive formulation of the statement: "*Stop moving, if I am not moving*" and covers the basic insight, that the correction of a wrong bearing must only happen while the user is moving in order to make it unobtrusive and invisible to the user that a correction is currently happening. To achieve this, the following interpolation was used:

$$\text{Improved Orientation Sensor 2} = \text{Orientation}_{Gyroscope} \oplus \qquad (5.2)$$
$$\text{Orientation}_{RotationVector} \cdot \text{Velocity}_{Gyroscope}$$

with

$$\text{Velocity}_{Gyroscope} = \text{Gyroscope}_X + \text{Gyroscope}_Y + \text{Gyroscope}_Z \qquad (5.3)$$

This approach mainly relies on the gyroscope but starts correcting, as soon as the user starts rotating the device. If the gyroscope drifted off but the user stops moving the incorrect pose will be preserved, until the user starts moving again. This might lead to a slightly wrong estimation but outperforms many other approaches in terms of stability and responsiveness. This approach is preferable for applications where stability is more important than absolute correctness, e.g. in AR games.

5.4.3 Further Issues

Another implementational issue should be mentioned: On some devices, the orientation sensor "jumps" when tilting the device but quickly goes back to the correct value when stopping. Fig. 5.4 illustrates the problem. When tilting the device, point A should move directly to point B (green line) but instead it jumps to the left, before converging to B (red line).

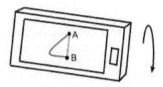

Figure 5.4: "Jumping" of the orientation sensor on some Android devices.

This artifact has a dramatic impact especially onto the second sensor fusion (equation 5.2) because those outliers (red path) will be used to correct the current rotation while in motion, whereas the true value is not being considered when the tilting ends because correction only takes place while in motion.

To overcome this issue, a simple *Jump filter* was introduced that detects exactly this case. Initially both quaternions (4-dimensional vectors) are initialised with the same values, so the dot-product between those vectors is exactly one. When slowly drifting off, this value will decrease moderately but if one of the two vectors suddenly jumps, the dot-product will drop too. If the dot-product falls below a certain threshold ϵ (e.g. 0.85), the fusion will fall back to the gyroscope only.

The Jump filter detects and removes outliers but introduced another problem at the same time. If a gyroscope failure occurs (e.g. due to heavy shaking) and the two virtual sensors are completely pointing towards different directions, the dot-product will always be below ϵ and no correction will happen anymore at all. But also this case can be detected relatively easy. When the dot-product falls below ϵ and the Jump filter is triggered, a counter (called *Panic counter*) will be increased by one and reset to zero if the dot-product is back above ϵ. If the Panic counter reaches a certain threshold n (e.g. 60) which means that the Jump filter was active for n consecutive measurements, both sensors have very likely diverged and a re-initialisation will be performed that resets the current state to the value of the orientation sensor.

When written in pseudocode, the Jump and Panic filter including the fusion can be expressed as

```
// Determine SLERP-weight
if(ImprovedOrientationSensor1) {
  // Use Improved Orientation Sensor 1
  // with constant correction
  w = 0.995; // Constant weight, close to 1
} else if (ImprovedOrientationSensor2) {
  // Use Improved Orientation Sensor 2
  // with velocity-dependent correction
  w = GyroVelocity_x + GyroVelocity_y + GyroVelocity_z;
}


// Jump filter
if (dot-product(Quat_Gyro, Quat_RotationVector) < epsilon) {
  // Only use Gyroscope and ignore RotationVector
  Quat_Fused = Quat_Gyro
  PanicCounter ++
} else {
  PanicCounter = 0
  // Perform regular SLERP
  Quat_Fused = SLERP(Quat_Gyro, Quat_RotationVector, w)
}


// Panic filter
if (PanicCounter > n) {
  // Reset to RotationVector and ignore Gyroscope
  Quat_Fused = Quat_RotationVector
}
```

Listing 5.1: Pseudocode implementation of Improved Orientation Sensor including Jump and Panic filter

One last remark: The above described sensor fusion requires the orientation sensor (Rotation Vector) to be reliable in order to perform a valid correction. Especially when coming close to objects that emit a strong magnetic field or if the compass is uncalibrated, the orientation sensor might not point towards magnetic north and the entire system will fail because it will constantly try to correct towards the wrong north.

6 Evaluation

This chapter starts with an extensive evaluation of different feature detectors, descriptors and matching-algorithms that are generally used in any CV-system and although the final system does not contain a computer-vision part, this evaluation gives useful advice which algorithms are well-suited and which algorithms are not.

During development, the results were visually verified by running a cube-visualisation that rotates accordingly to the movement of the device (see fig. 6.1). It can be downloaded from: https://bitbucket.org/apacha/sensor-fusion-demo.

The presented sensor fusion was furthermore evaluated against a second, reliable tracking system that delivers 6-DOF inside-out tracking from four infrared-cameras and served as ground-truth.

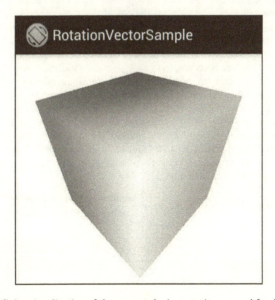

Figure 6.1: Cube-visualisation of the current device rotation as used for development and visual evaluation.

6.1 Evaluation of Feature Detectors, Descriptors and Matchers

Regardless of the approach, if computer-vision is used, feature-detection, feature-description and feature-matching are always present. The extent and form might differ and some systems use highly optimised algorithms (e.g. [Hofmann.2012]) but nevertheless the choice of the algorithm is not always clear. Therefore, this chapter gives an overview of different algorithms and how they perform. The entire source-code and results described in this chapter can be found and downloaded from https://bitbucket.org/apacha/cv-performance-evaluation. The performance was evaluated on a 64-bit Windows Laptop with an i5-2410M CPU running at 2.30 GHz and equipped with 8 GB RAM.

6.1.1 Feature Detectors

To evaluate the performance of a feature detector, the experiment shown in figure 6.2 was designed: Every algorithm (SIFT, SURF, ...) has to perform wide-baseline matching on a test-set of 60 images (resolution 1000x786px) that contains 10 different scenes and six images each with certain transformations like rotation, scaling, blurring, change in viewpoint or combinations of those [fig. 6.2, centre top]. The images were taken from [Mikolajczyk.2005][1] with two additional urban scenes from Christchurch that can be found in the repository linked above.

Each scene has one reference-image and five transformed images. The relationship between those pairs (the homography) was determined in advance and is known (fig. 6.2, top right). The first two measured metrics: runtime and number of detected features (fig. 6.2, left) are simply timed and counted during the evaluation. But to evaluate the reproducibility (fig. 6.2, bottom right), the detected features in the transformed images need to be reprojected back (fig. 6.2, right upper box) into the original image with the known homography and then compared with the features detected there (fig. 6.2, right lower box). If the original image contains a feature point at the same position with a small error ϵ, we call it a match. The reproducibility is then calculated as

$$\text{Reproducibility Score } (\%) = \frac{\text{Number of features detected}}{\text{Number of features matched}} \qquad (6.1)$$

---

[1]The data can be downloaded from http://www.robots.ox.ac.uk/~vgg/research/affine/

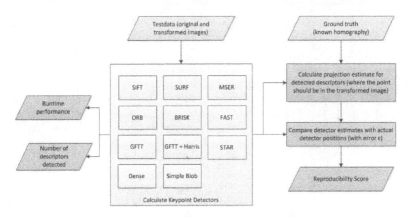

Figure 6.2: Experiment design of the feature detector evaluation

Table 6.1 gives an overview of evaluated feature detection algorithms that are implemented in OpenCV and their evaluation scores. The reproducibility score was calculated with different values for ϵ and the best results are shown. It clearly shows that the feature detectors FAST, STAR, ORB and Brinay Robust Invariant Scalable Keypoints (BRISK) clearly outperform other detectors.

Since the even distribution of feature points throughout the entire image is relevant for further steps, OpenCV offers the GridFeature-option that ensures that points are distributed evenly, which stands in conflict to many algorithms that try to find the most prominent spots (e.g. corners), even if they all clustered in a small region of the image.

Detector Name	Runtime per frame (ms)	Average Number of Keypoints	Best Reproducibility Score (%)	Remarks
Dense	67	16892	63	Detects a vast number of dense points in the image that are averagely spread, rather than a few interesting points.
FAST [Rosten.2010]	100	14872	55	Very fast with a high number of points that can be ranked by their score.
ORB [Rublee.2011]	133	497	42	Same as FAST, but only uses fixed number of best points (e.g. 500)
STAR [Agrawal.2008]	150	834	55	Very fast with high reproducibility
BRISK [Leutenegger.2011]	200	1388	46	Fast with good reproducibility
MSER [Matas.2004]	500	648	43	Medium performance; no ranking possible
Blob	500	14	54	Too few points detected
GFTT [Shi.1994]	900	1000	49	Slow performance for mobile applications
GFTT Harris	900	931	51	Slow performance for mobile applications
SURF [Bay.2006]	1100	5237	49	Performance too slow for mobile applications
SIFT [Lowe.2004]	1750	4900	46	Performance too slow for mobile applications

Table 6.1: Evaluation results for different feature detectors

6.1.2 Feature Descriptors

Different feature descriptors have been proposed, ranging from high-dimensional vectors like SIFT to more efficient binary descriptors such as ORB or FREAK. For a mobile application, performance is clearly an important criteria, so the runtime for different descriptors was evaluated in this part and is listed in table 6.2.

Descriptor Name	Type	Runtime for ~ 500 ORB features per frame (ms)	Runtime for ~ 5200 SURF features per frame (ms)
SIFT	128-dim Vector	3333	41683
SURF	64/128-dim Vector	1616	6083
BRISK	Binary	633	716
BRIEF [Calonder.2010]	Binary	50	550
ORB	Binary	67	83
FREAK [Alahi.2012]	Binary	100	233

Table 6.2: Evaluation results for different feature descriptors

To summarise table 6.2, binary feature descriptors are much faster to compute, so ORB, FREAK and BRIEF are more suitable for mobile application, where low computational cost is crucial. Especially ORB and FREAK clearly outperform high-dimensional descriptors like SURF and SIFT in terms of required time to compute.

6.1.3 Feature Matchers

The right choice of the matching-algorithm can have a huge impact on the performance, especially if descriptors are repeatedly matched against a huge database of more than 10.000 descriptors. However, for detector-descriptors-based tracking on a mobile phone, less than 500 features are usually detected, so brute-force algorithms dominate this evaluation, since they do not have an overhead of creating a matching database (like a kd-tree or a hash-index) that would be discarded in the next frame anyway.

It might also prove useful to find the n best matches for each feature point, if the IMU can provide an estimation, of where the matching point should be, the best point can easily be selected from this list. To evaluate this, a k-Nearest Neighbour (kNN) matching was performed with k=1 (nearest neighbour) and k=3 (three best neighbours). The runtime evaluation is given in table 6.3 and shows that for a small number of features (<10,000) brute-force matching is the most efficient and that there is no difference between performing a kNN-search with k=1 or k=3.

The third and fourth column in table 6.3 contain average values from four different detector/descriptor-combinations: ORB/ORB, SURF/SURF, FAST/FREAK and FAST/ORB. One final remark: The hamming distance is only meaningful for binary descriptors which SURF is not; the corresponding cells therefore contain no content.

Matcher Type	Matcher Name	Runtime for matching 500 features per frame (ms) Nearest Neighbour matching	Runtime for matching 500 features per frame (ms) K-Nearest Neighbour matching (k=3)	Runtime for matching 5200 SURF features per frame (ms) Nearest Neighbour matching	Runtime for matching 5200 SURF features per frame (ms) K-Nearest Neighbour matching (k=3)
Generic Matcher	Brute-Force L2	16	15	2467	2150
	Brute-Force L1	11	10	2333	2033
	Brute-Force Hamming Distance 1	11	11	n.a.	n.a.
	Brute-Force Hamming Distance 2	14	13	n.a.	n.a.
FLANN-based Matcher	FLANN-based	215	237	3167	3483
	Linear Brute Force	46	75	5533	6033
	KD Tree (randomised)	213	236	3100	3417
	K-Means (hierarchical)	78	89	2333	2133
	Composite (KD Tree and K-Means)	78	88	2300	2183
	Locality Sensitive Hashing (LSH)	526	550	n.a.	n.a.
	Autotuned	223	252	46583	45917

Table 6.3: Evaluation results for different feature matchers

6.1.4 Combining Detector, Descriptor and Matcher

This last part looks at the qualitative results of different combinations of feature detectors, descriptors and matching algorithms which in combination with the runtime-evaluation given above provides a clear recommendation, which algorithms perform best.

Since the choice of the matching algorithm (Generic matchers[2] as well as FLANN-based matchers[3] were evaluated) only has a major impact on the runtime but not on the quality, table 6.4 contains averaged values from all different matching algorithms.

The evaluation uses the same criterion as proposed in [Mikolajczyk.2005]. The same technique as for evaluating feature detectors is applied here as well. This allows to determine the number of correct matches (pairs that were found by the matching algorithm as well as by the ground-truth). Together with the total number of matches in the ground-truth and in the matching-algorithm the following formulas were used to calculate precision and recall:

$$\text{Precision} = \frac{\text{Number of correct matches}}{\text{Total number of matches from the matching algorithm}} \tag{6.2}$$

$$\text{Recall} = \frac{\text{Number of correct matches}}{\text{Total number of matches from the ground-truth}} \tag{6.3}$$

Precision can be interpreted as the percentage of correctly matched regions that can potentially contribute to the next step, e.g. a homography estimation. Recall is the number of correctly matched feature-pairs with respect to the total number of potential matches between two images of the same scene. The results are given in table 6.4.

Feature Detector	Feature Descriptor	Average Recall (%)	Average Precision (%)
ORB	ORB	0.193	0.357
BRISK	BRISK	0.206	0.684
FAST	FREAK	0.292	0.736
FAST	ORB	0.306	0.62
ORB	FREAK	0.29	0.4
SIFT	SIFT	0.323	0.643
SURF	SURF	0.299	0.633

Table 6.4: Evaluation results for different combinations of feature detectors and descriptors

---

[2]Generic matchers documentation: http://docs.opencv.org/modules/features2d/doc/common_interfaces_of_descriptor_matchers.html#descriptormatcher-create
[3]FLANN-based matchers documentation: http://docs.opencv.org/modules/flann/doc/flann_fast_approximate_nearest_neighbor_search.html#flann-index-t-index

Without surprises, SIFT/SIFT and SURF/SURF perform very well in terms of quality, but take magnitudes longer than more efficient algorithms. The clear winner in terms of quality and performance is the combination FAST/FREAK with one of the highest recall-rate and the highest precision while running faster than almost any other algorithm. The combinations FAST/ORB and BRISK/BRISK are also remarkably good. Interestingly ORB/ORB is significantly worse than FAST/ORB although the ORB feature detector uses FAST with an internal ranking, whereas in this performance evaluation, simply the 500 best FAST-features were selected (that had the highest response).

To conclude this evaluation, for detector-descriptor-based tracking on mobile phones, the FAST feature detector should be used in combination with FREAK feature descriptors and brute-force matching, running with 150-500 detected features per frame.

6.2 Strengths and limitations of IMU Sensor fusion

This chapter summarises the strengths and limitations of individual sensors and sensor fusion strategies. Table 6.5 contains my subjective impression of different approaches when running the Cube-Visualisation on different devices. Four tablets, three smartphones and Google Glass were used as hardware platform to run the application.

Sensors	Strengths	Limitations
Uncalibrated Gyroscope	+ Excellent dynamic response + Precise rotation-sensor	- No absolute orientation - Requires integration which leads to fast sensor drift
Accelerometer	+ Good dynamic response + Not deviated by magnetic noise	- Measures all accelerations including gravity
Compass	+ Measures magnetic north	- Slow response - Easily deviated from nearby magnetic fields
Gravity Sensor	+ Absolute orientation with respect to the ground	- No absolute orientation with respect to north
Linear Accelerometer	+ Measures pure accelerations of the device without gravity	- Heavy sensor drift if used for dead-reckoning
Calibrated Gyroscope	+ Excellent dynamic response + Precise rotation-sensor + Almost drift-free	- No absolute orientation - Failure under rapid motion
Accelerometer and Compass	+ Absolute orientation	- Jittering - High latency - Constant corrections (floating)
Orientation Sensor (Rotation Vector)	+ Good dynamic response + Absolute orientation	- Constant corrections (floating) - Jumps when tilting on some devices
Improved Orientation Sensor 1	+ Absolute orientation + Excellent dynamic response	- Slow but constant correction (floating)
Improved Orientation Sensor 2	+ Absolute orientation + Excellent dynamic response + No floating	- Does not perform correction if not moving, so the estimation might be slightly wrong (and is not corrected until the device starts moving again)

Table 6.5: Subjective perception of different sensors and sensor fusion approaches

6.3 Evaluation against VRPN Tracker

To evaluate the performance of the fusion algorithm, it was tested against a Virtual-Reality Peripheral Network (VRPN) tracker [TaylorII.2001] that was used as ground-truth while recording the sensor data from the mobile device at the same time. The VRPN system provides real-time 6-DOF position tracking and outputs position (3-dimensional vector) and orientation (4-dimensional Quaternion vector), so it can be compared almost directly to the measurements of the smartphone or the tablet. To perform outside-in marker-tracking, four spatially-aligned infrared cameras are used (see figure 6.3). The marker itself consists of five statically-aligned, light-reflecting balls that are attached to a pair of glasses (see figure 6.4).

Figure 6.3: Infrared camera that is used in the VRPN-tracking system

Although the VRPN tracker delivers 6-DOF tracking, only the rotational information was used, since the mobile tracking system only delivers 3-DOF rotation tracking. The evaluation was performed on two different devices: A Samsung Galaxy S2 and a Samsung Galaxy Tab 730. 8 data-sets of each approximately 60 seconds were generated with a similar motion pattern (see figure 6.5). The tables 6.6 and 6.7 refer to these data-sets as "Smartphone 1..5" and "Tablet 1..3".

The main challenge in this evaluation is the synchronisation between the two tracking systems: Both trackers start at different points in time, and have their events timestamped individually with varying time-intervals in between. After aligning the two data-sets temporally, the 3D rotations (Quaternions) need to be matched since

Figure 6.4: VRPN-marker that has five statically-aligned, light-reflecting balls attached to a pair of glasses.

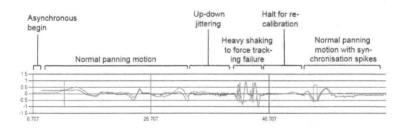

Figure 6.5: X-Axis of smartphone data-set 3 with motion-pattern explanations. Blue line represents X-component of the Quaternion as recorded by the mobile device, green line X-component of the Quaternion as recorded by the VRPN tracker and red vertical line indicates the synchronisation point.

it was not done before recording the data. This is done by selecting two very close measurements from both data-sets, finding the correlating transformation between them and applying the very same transformation to all data points in the second data-set. This process is done visually by verifying the results in a chart-diagram program that was developed for this purpose (see figure 6.6).

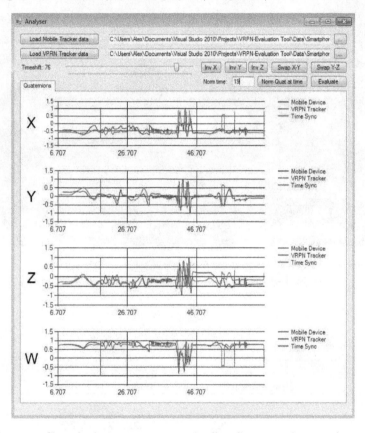

Figure 6.6: Chart-Analyser program to visually align two time-asynchronous datasets and evaluate difference.

Once the two data-sets are temporally and structurally aligned, a meaningful metric for rotations can be calculated, namely the angle difference between the ground-truth and the mobile device over time. To obtain this value, isochronic pairs of Quaternions are formed first. Then the Quaternion which transforms one into the other is calculated with equation 6.4 (which holds the rotational distance between them). Finally, the angle is extracted by converting it into axis-angle representation of which only the angle component is used.

$$\text{Quaternion}_{Transform} = \text{Quaternion}_1^{-1} \cdot \text{Quaternion}_2 \qquad (6.4)$$

This produces a list of approx. 3000 angle-pairs per data-set from which the deviation can be derived. The statistical results are given in table 6.6.

Dataset Name	Improved Orientation Sensor 1 deviation in °				Improved Orientation Sensor 2 deviation in °			
	Mean	SD	Median	MAD	Mean	SD	Median	MAD
Smart-phone 1	16.75	9.42	28.29	4.83	29.44	23.41	29.24	9.91
Smart-phone 2	19.26	8.4	33.14	4.26	23.21	12.49	31.34	7.16
Smart-phone 3	20.99	12.79	23.11	6.3	18.78	12.18	21.47	4.96
Smart-phone 4	40.48	30.96	38.1	17.13	18.83	10.03	26.11	6.54
Smart-phone 5	33.68	24.21	29.3	17.43	31.04	23.27	22.47	11.26
Tablet 1	21.15	9.57	24.02	6.6	36.53	32.76	23.62	10.42
Tablet 2	18.42	12.47	20.65	5.51	15.15	9.16	20.98	5.89
Tablet 3	12.42	10.01	18.35	3.28	10.04	7.59	15.54	3.3

Table 6.6: Qualitative evaluation results of sensor fusion performance against ground-truth. Values are statistical characteristics of the average deviation compared to VRPN tracker in degree over the entire test run.

Table 6.6 shows that the average deviation of the mobile rotation tracker compared to the VRPN tracker is between 10 and 40 degree deviation on the given dataset. But this test-set includes very difficult motions (including a forced tracking failure with reinitialisation). The results for normal motion are given in 6.7.

This concludes the evaluation and demonstrates the power of the sensor fusion algorithm that deviates from an expensive tracking system for normal motion only about 13-16 degree on average. Additionally it shows that the system is able to cope with difficult situations such as heavy shaking or a forced tracking failure by moving the device in a rapid eight-motion.

Dataset Name	Improved Orientation Sensor 1 deviation in °				Improved Orientation Sensor 2 deviation in °			
	Mean	SD	Median	MAD	Mean	SD	Median	MAD
Smart-phone 1	8.66	6.49	6.45	3.73	14.59	12.01	8.68	5.24
Smart-phone 2	14.8	8.9	22.2	5.23	16.58	12.07	21.56	7.4
Smart-phone 3	10.47	10.72	5.3	4.48	10.78	10.65	4.15	2.89
Smart-phone 4	18.12	13.02	17.59	11.25	4.19	3.35	3.17	2.68
Smart-phone 5	27.88	23.95	19.46	19.4	28.74	18.66	21.78	13.14
Tablet 1	18.95	7.96	25.91	3.85	18.86	11.44	21.04	6.53
Tablet 2	17.34	11.81	14.19	2.11	7.17	7.2	2.86	2.61
Tablet 3	8.46	9.29	4.97	4	6.13	6.26	4.9	3.86

Table 6.7: Qualitative evaluation results of sensor fusion performance against ground-truth. Values are statistical characteristics of the average deviation compared to VRPN tracker in degree over the first 25 seconds of each test run (that contains only normal motion).

7 Conclusion

If I have seen further it is by standing on the shoulders of giants.

Isaac Newton

The sensor fusion approach proposed in this thesis is a new approach of using the existing hardware of smartphones and tablet PCs in a better way to improve the quality of orientation estimations. The novelty of the sensor fusion is that it is based on the results of previous sensor fusion. It uses virtual instead of hardware sensors and builds another sensor fusion on top of it. This has not been done before and delivers convincing results that many applications can profit from.

However, the ultimate goal is to improve the process even further by including the visual sensors into the sensor fusion. But due to the limited time available, this thesis only contains a theoretical concept, how a system could look like that uses all sensors and what pitfalls lie ahead. Currently the camera is only used for visual augmentation but not for tracking the user-motion. At least future systems can build on top of the improved results from this thesis and even if used without the visual sensor (camera) the fusion provides better estimations than other IMU-only systems on a mobile phone. It delivers very stable results with an excellent dynamic response. The two different sensor fusion modes can be used in different scenarios. The first - more general - fusion can be seen as an improved, more robust and stable version of the existing orientation-sensor. The second fusion on the other hand is extremely stable and can be implemented into applications where accuracy is not as important as stability, like in games that utilise the smartphone as pointing device.

One problem that every system encounters, that uses a magnetic compass in its fusion is that of magnetic noise which can deflect the compass and corrupt the entire fusion. As a result, the proposed sensor fusion approach does not work if an electrical devices in nearby that emits a strong magnetic field.

The algorithms described in this thesis are implemented into the Mobile AR framework by the HitLab NZ but to guarantee compatibility with the existing framework some further adoptions need to be done because of different representations (Quaternions vs. Euler Angles). Currently the Mobile AR framework and the sensor fusion is implemented only on Android platforms. However, it can easily be ported to other platforms such as iOS or Windows Phone.

Finally, there are some variables being used in the sensor fusion that were determined empirically. These variables, like the threshold for the jump-filter or the gyroscope can be further optimised, especially since different mobile devices are equipped with sensors of very varying quality. For higher-quality sensors, those thresholds might be loosened to provide more accurate results while tighter thresholds might be required to guarantee a smooth operation with poor sensors.

Bibliography

[Agrawal.2008] Motilal Agrawal, Kurt Konolige, and Morten Rufus Blas. Censure: Center surround extremas for realtime feature detection and matching. In David Forsyth, Philip Torr, and Andrew Zisserman, editors, *Computer Vision - ECCV 2008*, volume 5305 of *Lecture Notes in Computer Science*, pages 102–115. Springer Berlin Heidelberg, Berlin and Heidelberg, 2008.

[AitAider.2006] Omar Ait-Aider, Nicolas Andreff, Jean Marc Lavest, and Philippe Martinet. Simultaneous object pose and velocity computation using a single view from a rolling shutter camera. In David Hutchison, Takeo Kanade, and Josef Kittler, editors, *Computer Vision - ECCV 2006*, volume 3952, pages 56–68. Springer Berlin Heidelberg, Berlin and Heidelberg, 2006.

[Alahi.2012] A. Alahi, R. Ortiz, and P. Vandergheynst. Freak: Fast retina keypoint. In *2012 IEEE Conference on Computer Vision and Pattern Recognition (CVPR)*, pages 510–517, 2012.

[Arulampalam.2002] M.S Arulampalam, S. Maskell, N. Gordon, and T. Clapp. A tutorial on particle filters for online nonlinear/non-gaussian bayesian tracking. *IEEE Transactions on Signal Processing*, 50(2):174–188, 2002.

[Azuma.1997] Ronald T. Azuma. A survey of augmented reality. 1997.

[Bay.2006] Herbert Bay, Tinne Tuytelaars, and Luc Gool. Surf: Speeded up robust features. In David Hutchison, Takeo Kanade, and Josef Kittler, editors, *Computer Vision - ECCV 2006*, volume 3951, pages 404–417. Springer Berlin Heidelberg, Berlin and Heidelberg, 2006.

[Bimber.2006] Oliver Bimber and Ramesh Raskar. Modern approaches to augmented reality, 2006.

[Bleser.2009] Gabriele Bleser and Didier Stricker. Advanced tracking through efficient image processing and visual–inertial sensor fusion. *Computers & Graphics*, 33(1):59–72, 2009.

[Bradski.2008] Gary R. Bradski and Adrian Kaehler. Learning opencv: Computer vision with the opencv library, 2008.

[Brown.2006] Leonard D. Brown and Hong Hua. Magic lenses for augmented virtual environments. *IEEE Computer Graphics and Applications*, 26(4):64–73, 2006.

[Calonder.2010] Michael Calonder, Vincent Lepetit, Christoph Strecha, and Pascal Fua. Brief: Binary robust independent elementary features. In David Hutchison, Takeo Kanade, and Josef Kittler, editors, *Computer Vision – ECCV 2010*, volume 6314 of *Lecture Notes in Computer Science*, pages 778–792. Springer Berlin Heidelberg, Berlin and Heidelberg, 2010.

[Choi.2012] C. Choi and H. I. Christensen. Robust 3d visual tracking using particle filtering on the special euclidean group: A combined approach of keypoint and edge features. *The International Journal of Robotics Research*, 31(4):498–519, 2012.

[Comport.2006] Andrew I. Comport, E. Marchand, M. Pressigout, and François Chaumette. Real-time markerless tracking for augmented reality: the virtual visual servoing framework. *IEEE Transactions on Visualization and Computer Graphics*, 12(4):615–628, 2006.

[Davison.2007] Andrew J. Davison, Ian D. Reid, Nicholas D. Molton, and Olivier Stasse. Monoslam: Real-time single camera slam. *IEEE Transactions on Pattern Analysis and Machine Intelligence*, 29(6):1052–1067, 2007.

[Dunser.2012] Andreas Dünser, Mark Billinghurst, James Wen, Vilma Lehtinen, and A. Nurminen. Exploring the use of handheld ar for outdoor navigation. *Computers and Graphics*, 36(8):1084–1095, 2012.

[Eck.2013] U. Eck and C. Sandor. Harp: A framework for visuo-haptic augmented reality. In *Virtual Reality (VR), 2013 IEEE*, pages 145–146, 2013.

[Feldman.2005] A. Feldman, E.M Tapia, S. Sadi, P. Maes, and C. Schmandt. Reachmedia: On-the-move interaction with everyday objects. In *Ninth IEEE International Symposium on Wearable Computers (ISWC'05)*, pages 52–59, 2005.

[Fritz.2005] F. Fritz, A. Susperregui, and Maria Teresa Linaza. Enhancing cultural tourism experience with augmented reality technologies. *The 6th International Symposium on Virtual Reality, Archaeology and Cultural Heritage VAST*, 2005.

[Furht.2011] Borko Furht, editor. *Handbook of Augmented Reality*. Springer New York, New York, 2011.

[Gauglitz.2011] Steffen Gauglitz, Tobias Höllerer, and Matthew Turk. Evaluation of interest point detectors and feature descriptors for visual tracking. *International Journal of Computer Vision*, 94(3):335–360, 2011.

[Harris.2013] Mark Harris. How new indoor navigation systems will protect emergency responders: Tracking firefighters in blazing buildings helps keep them safe, 2013.

[Hofmann.2012] Robert Hofmann, Hartmut Seichter, and Gerhard Reitmayr. A gpgpu accelerated descriptor for mobile devices. pages 289–290.

[JeroenHol.2008] Jeroen Hol. *Pose Estimation and Calibration Algorithms for Vision and Inertial Sensors*. PhD thesis, Linköping University, Sweden, 2008.

[Jiang.2004] B. Jiang, U. Neumann, and Suya You. A robust hybrid tracking system for outdoor augmented reality. In *IEEE Virtual Reality Proceedings 2004*, pages 3–275. 2004.

[Kato.1999] Hirokazu Kato and Mark Billinghurst. Marker tracking and hmd calibration for a video-based augmented reality conferencing system. In *Augmented Reality, 1999. (IWAR '99) Proceedings. 2nd IEEE and ACM International Workshop on*, pages 85–94, 1999.

[Klein.2004] Georg Klein and Tom W. Drummond. Tightly integrated sensor fusion for robust visual tracking. *Image and Vision Computing*, 22(10):769–776, 2004.

[Klein.2006] Georg Klein and David Murray. Full-3d edge tracking with a particle filter. 2006.

[Klein.2007] Georg Klein and David Murray. Parallel tracking and mapping for small ar workspaces. In *Proc. Sixth IEEE and ACM International Symposium on Mixed and Augmented Reality (ISMAR'07)*, pages 1–10, Nara and Japan, 2007.

[Klein.2009] Georg Klein. *Visual tracking for augmented reality: Edge-based tracking techniques for AR applications*. VDM Verl. Müller, Saarbrücken, 2009.

[Klein.2009b] Georg Klein and David Murray. Parallel tracking and mapping on a camera phone. In *Proc. Eigth IEEE and ACM International Symposium on Mixed and Augmented Reality (ISMAR'09)*, pages 83–86, Orlando, 2009.

[Kleinert.2012] Markus Kleinert and Uwe Stilla. On sensor pose parameterization for inertial aided visual slam. pages 1–9, 2012.

[Kounavis.2012] Chris D. Kounavis, Anna E. Kasimati, and Efpraxia D. Zamani. Enhancing the tourism experience through mobile augmented reality: Challenges and prospects. *International Journal of Engineering Business Management*, page 1, 2012.

[Kurz.2011]   D. Kurz and Selim Benhimane. Gravity-aware handheld augmented reality. In *2011 10th IEEE International Symposium on Mixed and Augmented Reality*, pages 111–120, 2011.

[Lawitzki.2012] Paul Lawitzki. *Application of Dynamic Binaural Signals in Acoustic Games*. PhD thesis, Stuttgart Media University, Stuttgart, 2012.

[Lee.2012]   Gun Lee and Mark Billinghurst. Cityviewar outdoor ar visualization, 2012.

[Lee.2013]   Gun Lee, Andreas Dünser, Alaeddin Nassani, and Mark Billinghurst. Antarcticar: An outdoor ar experience of a virtual tour to antarctica. In *IEEE International Symposium on Mixed and Augmented Reality 2013*. Adelaide, 2013.

[Lemaire.2007] Thomas Lemaire, Cyrille Berger, Il-Kyun Jung, and Simon Lacroix. Vision-based slam: Stereo and monocular approaches. *International Journal of Computer Vision*, 74(3):343–364, 2007.

[Leutenegger.2011] Stefan Leutenegger, Margarita Chli, and Roland Y. Siegwart. Brisk: Binary robust invariant scalable keypoints. In *2011 IEEE International Conference on Computer Vision (ICCV)*, pages 2548–2555, 2011.

[Lewis.2004]   John R. Lewis. In the eye of the beholder: Scanning light beams to the retina could revolutionize displays for everything from cellphones to games, 2004.

[Lindeman.2012] Robert W. Lindeman, Gun Lee, Leigh Beattie, Hannes Gamper, Rahul Pathinarupothi, and Aswin Akhilesh. Geoboids: A mobile ar application for exergaming. pages 93–94, 2012.

[Liu.2009]   Yue Liu and Yongtian Wang. Ar-view: An augmented reality device for digital reconstruction of yuangmingyuan. In *2009 IEEE International Symposium on Mixed and Augmented Reality 2009 - Arts, Media and Humanities*, pages 3–7, 2009.

[Livingston.2008] Mark A. Livingston and Zhuming Ai. The effect of registration error on tracking distant augmented objects. In *2008 7th IEEE/ACM International Symposium on Mixed and Augmented Reality (ISMAR)*, pages 77–86, 2008.

[LonguetHiggins.1987] H. C. Longuet-Higgins. A computer algorithm for reconstructing a scene from two projections. *Readings in Computer Vision: Issues, Problems, Principles, and Paradigms, MA Fischler and O. Firschein, eds*, pages 61–62, 1987.

[Lowe.2004] David G. Lowe. Distinctive image features from scale-invariant key-points. *International Journal of Computer Vision*, 60(2):91–110, 2004.

[Lucas.1981] Bruce D. Lucas and Takeo Kanade. An iterative image registration technique with an application to stereo vision. In *Proceedings of Imaging Understanding Workshop*, pages 121–130. 1981.

[Mahony.2008] Robert Mahony, Tarek Hamel, and Jean-Michel Pflimlin. Nonlinear complementary filters on the special orthogonal group. *IEEE Transactions on Automatic Control*, 53(5):1203–1218, 2008.

[Matas.2004] J. Matas, O. Chum, M. Urban, and T. Pajdla. Robust wide-baseline stereo from maximally stable extremal regions. *Image and Vision Computing*, 22(10):761–767, 2004.

[Mikolajczyk.2005] K. Mikolajczyk and C. Schmid. A performance evaluation of local descriptors. *IEEE Transactions on Pattern Analysis and Machine Intelligence*, 27(10):1615–1630, 2005.

[Milgram.1994] Paul Milgram and Fumio Kishino. A taxonomy of mixed reality visual displays. *IEICE Transactions on Information Systems*, (Vol E77-D, No.12), 1994.

[Newcombe.2011] Richard A. Newcombe, Steven J. Lovegrove, and Andrew J. Davison. Dtam: Dense tracking and mapping in real-time. In *2011 IEEE International Conference on Computer Vision (ICCV)*, pages 2320–2327, 2011.

[Oskiper.2013] Taragay Oskiper, Mikhail Sizintsev, Vlad Branzoi, Supun Samarasekera, and Rakesh Kumar. Augmented reality binoculars. In *IEEE International Symposium on Mixed and Augmented Reality 2013*. Adelaide, 2013.

[Ozuysal.2007] Mustafa Ozuysal, Pascal Fua, and Vincent Lepetit. Fast keypoint recognition in ten lines of code. In *2007 IEEE Conference on Computer Vision and Pattern Recognition*, pages 1–8, 2007.

[Papagiannakis.2008] George Papagiannakis, Gurminder Singh, and Nadia Magnenat-Thalmann. A survey of mobile and wireless technologies for augmented reality systems. *Computer Animation and Virtual Worlds*, 19(1):3–22, 2008.

[Pinies.2007] Pedro Pinies, Todd Lupton, Salah Sukkarieh, and Juan D. Tardos. Inertial aiding of inverse depth slam using a monocular camera. 2007.

[Pirchheim.2013] Christian Pirchheim, Dieter Schmalstieg, and Gerhard Reitmayr. Handling pure camera rotation in keyframe-based slam. In *IEEE International Symposium on Mixed and Augmented Reality 2013*. Adelaide, 2013.

[Randeniya.2008] Duminda Randeniya, Manjriker Gunaratne, and Sudeep Sarkar. Fusion of vision inertial data for automatic georeferencing. In Auroop Ganguly, João Gama, Olufemi Omitaomu, Mohamed Medhat Gaber, and Ranga Raju Vatsavai, editors, *Knowledge Discovery from Sensor Data*, volume 20083859 of *Industrial Innovation*, pages 107–130. CRC Press, 2008.

[Reitmayr.2003] Gerhard Reitmayr and Dieter Schmalstieg. Location based applications for mobile augmented reality. pages 65–73, 2003.

[Rolland.2001] Jannick P. Rolland, Yohan Baillot, and Alexei A. Goon. A survey of tracking technology for virtual environments. pages 67–112, 2001.

[Rosten.2010] E. Rosten, R. Porter, and T. Drummond. Faster and better: A machine learning approach to corner detection. *IEEE Transactions on Pattern Analysis and Machine Intelligence*, 32(1):105–119, 2010.

[Rublee.2011] Ethan Rublee, Vincent Rabaud, Kurt Konolige, and Gary Bradski. Orb: An efficient alternative to sift or surf. In *2011 IEEE International Conference on Computer Vision (ICCV)*, pages 2564–2571, 2011.

[Rusu.2011] Radu Bogdan Rusu and Steve Cousins. 3d is here: Point cloud library (pcl). In *IEEE International Conference on Robotics and Automation (ICRA)*, Shanghai and China, 2011.

[Schall.2009] Gerhard Schall, Daniel Wagner, Gerhard Reitmayr, Elise Taichmann, Manfred Wieser, Dieter Schmalstieg, and Bernhard Hofmann-Wellenhof. Global pose estimation using multi-sensor fusion for outdoor augmented reality. In *2009 IEEE International Symposium on Mixed and Augmented Reality 2009 - Arts, Media and Humanities*, pages 153–162, 2009.

[Schon.2007] Thomas B. Schon, Rickard Karlsson, David Tornqvist, and Fredrik Gustafsson. A framework for simultaneous localization and mapping utilizing model structure. In *2007 10th International Conference on Information Fusion*, pages 1–8, 2007.

[Shi.1994] Jianbo Shi and Carlo Tomasi. Good features to track. In *IEEE Conference on Computer Vision and Pattern Recognition*, pages 593–600, 1994.

[Shoemake.1985] Ken Shoemake. Animating rotation with quaternion curves. *SIGGRAPH '85*, pages 245–254, 1985.

[Skrypnyk.2004] I. Skrypnyk and D.G Lowe. Scene modelling, recognition and tracking with invariant image features. *Proceedings of the Third IEEE and ACM International Symposium on Mixed and Augmented Reality*, pages 110–119, 2004.

[Sodhi.2013] Rajinder Sodhi, Ivan Poupyrev, Matthew Glisson, and Ali Israr. Aireal: Interactive tactile experiences in free air. In *SIGGRAPH '13*. Anaheim and CA and USA, 2013.

[Steux.2010] Bruno Steux and Oussama El Hamzaoui. tinyslam: A slam algorithm in less than 200 lines c-language program. In *Vision (ICARCV 2010)*, pages 1975–1979, 2010.

[Tamaazousti.2011] Mohamed Tamaazousti, Vincent Gay-Bellile, Sylvie Naudet Collette, and Steve Bourgeois. Real-time accurate localization in a partially known environment: Application to augmented reality on textureless 3d objects, 2011.

[Tan.2013] Wei Tan, Haomin Liu, Zilong Dong, Guofeng Zhang, and Hujun Bao. Robust monocular slam in dynamic environments. In *IEEE International Symposium on Mixed and Augmented Reality 2013*. Adelaide, 2013.

[TaylorII.2001] Russell M. Taylor II, Thomas C. Hudson, Adam Seeger, Hans Weber, Jeffrey Juliano, and Aron T. Helser. Vrpn: A device-independent, network-transparent vr peripheral system. 2001.

[Vlahakis.2002] V. Vlahakis, M. Ioannidis, J. Karigiannis, M. Tsotros, M. Gounaris, D. Stricker, T. Gleue, P. Daehne, and L. Almeida. Archeoguide: an augmented reality guide for archaeological sites. *IEEE Computer Graphics and Applications*, 22(5):52–60, 2002.

[Wagner.2007] Daniel Wagner. *Handheld Augmented Reality*. PhD thesis, TU Graz, Graz and Austria, 2007.

[Wagner.2008] Daniel Wagner, Gerhard Reitmayr, Alessandro Mulloni, Tom W. Drummond, and Dieter Schmalstieg. Pose tracking from natural features on mobile phones. In *2008 7th IEEE/ACM International Symposium on Mixed and Augmented Reality (ISMAR)*, pages 125–134, 2008.

[Wang.2009] Patricia P. Wang, Tao Wang, Dayong Ding, Yimin Zhang, Wenyuan Bi, and Yingze Bao. Mirror world navigation for mobile users based on augmented reality. page 1025, 2009.

[Welch.2006] Greg Welch and Gary Bishop. *An Introduction to the Kalman Filter*. PhD thesis, University of North Carolina at Chapel Hill, 2006.

[Weng.2006] Shiuh-Ku Weng, Chung-Ming Kuo, and Shu-Kang Tu. Video object tracking using adaptive kalman filter. *Journal of Visual Communication and Image Representation*, 17(6):1190–1208, 2006.

Appendix

List of Abbreviations

AR Augmented Reality

AV Augmented Virtuality

BRISK Brinay Robust Invariant Scalable Keypoints

CAD Computer Aided Design

CV Computer Vision

DGPS Differential Global Positioning System

DOF Degrees-of-Freedom

DTAM Dense Tracking and Mapping

FAST Features from Accelerated Segment Test

FREAK Fast Retina Keypoint

GLONASS Globalnaja nawigazionnaja sputnikowaja sistema (rus.)

GNSS Global Navigation Satellite System

GPS Global Positioning System

HMD Head-Mounted Display

IMU Inertial Measurement Unit

KLT Kanade-Lucas-Tomasi

kNN k-Nearest Neighbour

ORB Oriented FAST and Rotated BRIEF

PDA Personal Digital Assistant

PTAM Parallel tracking and mapping

RANSAC Random Sample Consensus

RTK Real Time Kinematic

SAD Sum of Absolute Differences

SDK Software Development Kit

SLAM Simultaneous Localisation and mapping

SLERP Spherical Linear Interpolation

SIFT Scale Invariant Feature Transform

SURF Speeded-Up robust features

UTM Universal Transverse Mercator

VR Virtual Reality

VRPN Virtual-Reality Peripheral Network

Index